ASTRAL
PROJECTION

ASTRAL PROJECTION

A Record of Out-of-the-Body Experiences

Oliver Fox

E P B M

ECHO POINT BOOKS & MEDIA, LLC

Published in 2016 by Echo Point Books & Media
Brattleboro, Vermont
www.EchoPointBooks.com

Astral Projection
ISBN: 978-1-62654-800-8 (paperback)
978-1-62654-801-5 (casebound)

Cover image: Andrew Spencer,
Courtesy of Unsplash

Cover design by Justine McFarland,
Editorial and proofreading assistance by Ian Straus,
Echo Point Books & Media

To my Wife

O Soul, thou quivering, radiant bird !
   Wing from thy prison-house : God bids thee speed.
Wisdom and love beyond the spoken word
   Await thee, freed.

FOREWORD

I owe my knowledge of this book to Hereward
Carrington. In his introduction to Sylvan Muldoon's
book on the same subject, Dr. Carrington says of it:
"The only detailed, scientific and first-hand account
of a series of conscious and voluntarily controlled
astral projections which I have ever come across is
that by Mr. Oliver Fox, published in the *Occult
Review* for 1920." This is high praise, indeed. It sent
me in search of the original articles, which I found
well worth reading. This was in 1929, shortly after
Mr. Muldoon's book appeared. But, it was not until
quite recently that I discovered – apparently it had
been published in the dark of the moon – that Oliver
Fox had later expanded his articles into a book,
which you now have before you. The book itself
bears no date of publication. But, as the reader will
note on page 117, there is a comment by the author
dated March 1, 1938, so that the book must have
been published thereafter. It appears to have been
published just the once, in England. This is the first
time it is published in the United States.

If I had any control over the situation, I would
prefer not to use the term "Astral Projection." Much
more simple and accurate is to use the term "Out of
Body Experiences." As far as I have been able to

ascertain, Oliver Fox, himself, never uses the term "Astral Projection." His original articles in the *Occult Review* in 1920, for which he is justly considered the pioneer in this field, were entitled "The Pineal Doorway," and "Beyond the Pineal Door." (As he explains in this book, one should not think that he is using the term *pineal* anatomically.) In the text of this book, too, I find no passage in which he speaks of it as "Astral Projection." I think the term was imposed upon him by his English publisher, in imitation of the term used by Sylvan Muldoon. The point is that the term, "Astral Body," which was made so popular by Mr. Muldoon, properly belongs to the doctrine of Theosophy, where it has quite another meaning, being one of five bodies, and not at all the most spiritual. One must recognize, however, that at least for the present Mr. Muldoon's use of the term "Astral Projection" is the one most familiar to people today, and one will have to be content with it.

In this use of the term, the Astral Body is the Double, or the ethereal counterpart of the physical body, which it resembles and with which it normally coincides. Each of us has one. There is quite a substantial body of cases in the literature of psychic research concerning instances in which a person found himself having an Out of the Body experience. Sometimes it arose out of a very serious accident. Sometimes it came in the course of a profound illness. At other times it resulted from a shock of tragic information or a harrowing experience. The interested reader will find a quick summary of all this in Hereward Carrington's introduction to Sylvan

Muldoon's book. Those who wish to go further will find a considerable amount of material in two books that we have published: F. W. H. Myers' *Human Personality and its Survival of Bodily Death* and Mrs. Sidgwick's *Phantasms of the Living.* There is also a short section, giving typical cases, in G. N. M. Tyrrell's *Science & Psychical Phenomena & Apparitions,* which he entitles "Out-of-the-body" experiences.

All these cases include very little conscious, experimental work in inducing out of the body experiences. It is for this conscious, experimental approach that Sylvan Muldoon is justly famous in his *The Projection of the Astral Body.* Much less well known, as I have indicated, is the work of Oliver Fox which, in the form of the *Occult Review* articles, preceded Muldoon's work.

There is an almost excessive modesty in Mr. Fox's writings on this subject. It is plain that he feels deeply the need not to underline those of his experiences which carry more evidential weight than the others, he records his failures and inconsequential experiences at well nigh equal length. As a matter of fact, the reader accustomed to other, boastful accounts is likely to go back to the beginning of this introduction and read again with some puzzlement Hereward Carrington's strong praise of this book. But the patient reader, and above all the genuinely interested reader, will in the end awake to the fact that under the seemingly casual description of his experiments, Mr. Fox provides a quite precise methodology for inducing out of the body experiences. How unique this is in the literature is known to those of us who have had to chew a great deal of straw without result.

As he tells us, Mr. Fox has avoided as much as possible anything not pertaining quite directly to the problem of out of the body experiences. Inevitably, however, he has had to indicate his own Theosophical background. But we can share his experiments and experiences without embracing his Theosophical views. There is common ground on the question of out of the body experiences for people of the most varied religious views or no religious views. To put it even more plainly, out of the body experiences are *facts* no matter how each one of us explains them to himself. No genuinely open minded person has questioned this since Myers' *Human Personality* and Mrs. Sidgwick's *Phantasms of the Living*. One can still, of course, question the technique for inducing them offered by Oliver Fox. But whatever one's final conclusion, his technique merits our study. The fascinating point, to which my mind returns, and to which the mind of any serious reader must likewise return, is the uniqueness of Mr. Fox's account of his technique.

JOHN C. WILSON

CONTENTS

CHAPTER I

In view of the peculiar interest dreams were to have for me later on in life, I think it would be well to start this record right back in the days when I was very young and the jolly little horse-trams, with their cheerful bells, clattered past my home in the Seven Sisters Road. Some points of importance will be brought to light, though naturally many years were to pass before their significance could be appreciated by me. Also it may help to settle the question as to whether my projection experiments have been made possible by some congenital psychic abnormality ; but it must be remembered that, although generally dismissed as nonsense and make-believe, psychic experiences are by no means uncommon in early childhood.

As a child I progressed from illness to illness—in truth, the first words I can remember hearing are, "It's the croup again"—and life was often temporarily arrested for me by monotonous spells of bed, though enlivened by exceedingly hot poultices and very nasty medicine. Yes, I was certainly delicate and highly strung. Although not originally intended to serve this purpose, a brass cross let into the pavement outside Holyrood Church, Southampton, still marks the spot where I once lay on my back and kicked, to the embarrassment of my mother and the detriment of my nice white sailor-suit. From which it may be inferred that I was also a little temperamental.

On looking back, it seems to me that in those early days, until I was seven or eight years old, my dreams were chiefly of the nightmare variety. I suppose there must have been happy ones too ; but with a few exceptions these have made no permanent impression on my memory, and I know that when I went to bed I was afraid of dreaming. Most of these nightmares were of the ordinary kind ; but there were two of a recurrent type that have a very special bearing on our subject of astral projection.

The first of these I have named the dream of the Double. In this dream my mother and I would be sitting together in the dining-room ; and nearly always it was evening, and the oil-lamp would be burning and perhaps a cosy fire blazing on the hearth. At first things seemed quite normal, but soon a strange change came over the peaceful scene. My mother would stop talking and stare fixedly at me with her beautiful, compelling eyes, and at the same time the lamplight and the firelight would grow dim, while another light—golden and coming seemingly from nowhere—filled the room. Then the door would open and another mother, dressed in exactly the same way to the smallest detail, would enter and walk towards me ; and she, too, stared silently with beautiful, mesmeric eyes. Then the awful dream-fear swept over me ; and after the usual struggle to cry out, I would wake, actually screaming.

Now, my mother—whom I was fated to lose so soon, for she died when I was thirteen—seemed the most lovely thing in my world. Why, then, should I be overcome with terror because there were two of her? True, this happening was contrary to the ordinary run of events in waking life, but miraculous things frequently occurred in my dreams without frightening me, being taken for granted and not recognized as abnormal while I was still dreaming. It seemed to me at the time, and for many years after, that my fear found its origin in this dilemma: I was confronted with two mothers, as alike as two peas, and I could not tell which was my *real* mother. Yet why should this uncertainty produce such panic? I incline now to the view that these "double" dreams were different from the ordinary nightmare, that my body was in a deeper state of trance than is usual with normal sleep, and that some degree of separation had occurred, so that my consciousness became invaded by the terrible unreasoning fear so often associated with this trance condition.

During childhood the dream of the Double occurred, I should think, three or four times a year, though at irregular intervals. While my mother lived she nearly always figured in it, though occasionally the scene would be different and her place taken by my father or some other relative or friend. I cannot now be sure if I ever dreamed of her in this way after her death, but this dream became gradually rarer and rarer, and I have not had it now for many years. Just once my wife was the principal character, and once I saw my own double. In the latter case I seemed to glimpse my Twin of Darkness, for I looked very old and incredibly evil ; but it is interesting to note that, though shocked by the wicked appearance of my double, I did not feel afraid of it.

The other nightmare, which I regard as having peculiar significance, was much rarer and took many forms, though the same underlying principle was manifest in each. I have called it the fear of Extension. The earliest example I can remember of this dream is an unending procession of coal-men emptying sacks of coal on to a pile which slowly grows higher and higher. Something in me seems to be linked with the mounting black column and is gradually being stretched tighter and tighter. There is a terrible sense of fate, of inevitability : the coal-men will never cease emptying their sacks, the black column will never cease mounting to the sky, and the torment in me will grow and grow until. . . ? Then follows panic, the struggle to cry out, and the breaking of the dream.

The last example of this dream that I can remember occurred when I was about eighteen. I dreamed that my grandfather and I were sitting at the supper-table. Suddenly he took a threepenny-bit from his pocket and held it between his finger and thumb across the table for me to see. "A little threepenny-bit !" he exclaimed, "but it will grow and grow and grow and nothing can ever stop it !" His voice grew steadily louder until it ended in a scream : "It will grow and grow and grow until it cuts the world in two !" Now, in my dream, though the threepenny-bit did not increase in size, something in me seemed linked with an invisible coin and was being stretched as it grew larger and larger in obedience to my grandfather's horrible monologue. There was the same awful sense of inevitability and helplessness, ending in panic. I echoed his scream, and that broke the nightmare.

When I was very small, about four or five, this Extension dream would intrude now and then upon my waking life. Like most children, I would at times fall into a reverie when playing with my toys and just sit staring at nothing in particular. Suddenly a subtle change would come over the room, though everything looked the same, and I would begin to feel frightened. I could not understand the nature of this change and could only explain it to my small self by saying that "things went wrong". I might have, say, one hand resting on the table and one on the back of my chair. The illusion was that I could not remove my hands and that the table and chair were very slowly separating and stretching me, yet at the same time I knew with one part of my mind that they were not *really* moving. It was perhaps this knowledge that prevented the fear reaching nightmare dimensions and ending in panic. I would struggle to remove my hands and then, just as suddenly, things would "come right" again. I was free, but very bewildered as to what had happened to me. On one occasion, when my hands were resting on the crocheted cover to my play-box, the network seemed to be expanding and separating my fingers. When things "went wrong", whether by daylight or lamplight, the light changed in a way similar to that described in the dream of the Double.

I think that these Extension nightmares also were

probably the result of an abnormal physical state—the
body being in an unusually deep trance—and invaded
by the fear peculiar to that condition.   Here, too,
some degree of separation of the vehicles may have
taken place, the exteriorization arousing in my consciousness the idea of strain or extension.   The waking
Extension experiences were obviously produced by
self-hypnosis.

At this stage it is just possible that some of my
readers of a psycho-analytical turn of mind may be
tempted to remark : "This chap Fox seems to have
knocked the bottom out of his projection experiments
already !   In early childhood he was dominated by the
ideas of the Double and Extension, and all the rest
follows from these two facts.   His seeming out-of-the-
body adventures have been purely imaginary."

Well, if I were the *only* person to have had such
experiences, this line of criticism would be worthy of
serious attention, though even then I think it would
be very difficult to make psycho-analysis cover all the
facts of the case.   However, one has only to turn to
The Mystery of the Human Double, by the Hon. Ralph
Shirley, to see what a large amount of corroborative
evidence has followed the publication of my article,
"The Pineal Doorway", in the *Occult Review* for April,
1920.   While in my opinion the experiences narrated
in this chapter are of undoubted interest for the light
they throw upon my psychic constitution, I do not
think they can fairly be said to invalidate the results
of my research.   Personally, I am disposed to look to
my horoscope, to which I refer later, for the true
explanation of those forces which were to manifest in

my life, producing first the Double and Extension dreams and later the experiments which form the subject of this book.

Sometimes, just before falling asleep, I would see through my closed eyelids a number of small misty-blue or mauve vibrating circles. Now I should describe this structure as somewhat resembling a mass of frog's eggs, and only just on the border line of visibility. At first these circles would be empty, but soon a tiny grinning face, with piercing steel-blue eyes, would appear in each circle, and I would hear a chorus of mocking voices saying very rapidly, as though in tune with the vibration, "That is it, you see ! That is it, you see !" Always they said the same thing, but I have never been able to trace the origin of these words or to fathom their meaning, if any. And as the appearance of these faces always heralded a par-ticularly nasty nightmare, I grew to dread their coming.

This state of things persisted for two or three years, though it must be remembered that it was only at irregular intervals of several weeks that I was able to see these circles, and then came a quite inexplicable happening. The vibrating circles appeared, empty at first, and lo and behold, they became filled by little glass ink-pots ! And there was no nightmare ! There-after I performed a feat of childish magic. When the empty circles came I would give the command, "Let it be ink-stands !" for I confused the pot with the stand in those days. Sure enough, the little glass pots would appear and there would be no nightmare. But I had to be very quick about it or the grinning faces would get in first, I would hear their nonsensical words, and the nightmare would follow in due course. This queer incident forms a good illustration of the power of suggestion, but it has a deeper significance also ; for in my out-of-the-body experiences I have noted on several occasions, beneath the golden glow suffusing the room, this barely visible, vibrating curtain of circular cells. I do not know what it is, but I believe it is always present at the back of things, if one concentrates upon it, though it will often remain unnoticed because of the more arresting nature of other phenomena. But in my projection experiences these vibrating circles remain empty. It was only in my early childhood that impish faces or friendly ink-pots appeared in them.

In the room where I slept there was what used to be called a fish-tail burner—now, like the lamplighter with his rod, a thing of the past. Through the clear glass of the globe I could see the bright, fan-shaped flame with its central cone of blackish purple, or dark blue, in which little red spots shot upwards. In my drowsy condition I used to watch these mounting spots as they traversed the dark space and became lost in the outer brightness, and sometimes things would suddenly "go wrong". The light of the gas-flame grew dim and that mysterious pale-golden light from nowhere suffused the room. I would hear strange noises, crackling and snapping noises, while little shafts of blue flame, like miniature lightning, darted from the corners of the room. And then came the apparition : a man with a grotesquely horrible face, a wolf with eyes of fire, a lion, a huge serpent, a great black bear standing erect so that it reached the ceiling —I saw all these at different times. And I just yelled and yelled. The apparition would stay quite still, glowering at me, and I could hear my mother running up the stairs in answer to my frantic S O S; but as soon as she turned the door-knob, the fearsome beast vanished and things "came right" again.

It must have been very irritating for my mother, but she was always sweet and gentle with me. She, of course, thought that I had been dreaming, and impressed upon me that it was only a nightmare. Well, I know now that it was not. These experiences, which were quite rare and probably finished with by the time I was six, were undoubtedly the result of self-induced trance caused by staring at the gas-flame. Such apparitions, lights and sounds are common happenings in that trance condition which forms the prelude to a conscious projection. There is one thing, however, which still puzzles me : I cannot understand why my shouts did not break the trance before my mother entered the room. It may be that my memory is unreliable in respect of the precise point at which the apparition vanished, but I do not feel that this is the explanation.

Just one experience of a pleasant nature falls into this category. A funny little fellow dressed in brown— rather like those garden gnomes one gets a little tired of seeing nowadays—clambered up on to my bed and smiled at me reassuringly. He pointed to a screen that stood near, and then a bright circle of light appeared which is now suggestive of a magic-lantern, although I do not think I had ever seen one at the time this happened. In this circle, from misty beginnings, was gradually evolved an enchanting, vividly coloured picture of a farmyard scene. And everything was *moving*. Horses, cows, dogs, etc., all moving; ducks swimming on the pond; and a woman in a blue dress waving her hand from the doorway of the farmhouse. Presently the picture faded away, the gnome vanished with a farewell nod and smile, and I was left apparently awake and greatly wondering. The chief point of interest here is the circle of light; for in the years to come I was to see it again, though without the gnome and the farmyard scene, and other investigators have noted a similar phenomenon.

I am tempted to relate one more experience of early childhood, though it has no bearing on the subject of projection. I was lying in bed in the daylight and feeling very disgruntled—perhaps I had been extra naughty and sent to bed earlier than usual. Life was a bore, parents were unjust, and going to sleep meant dreams and possibly bad ones. But there was nothing to be done about it, so I closed my eyes. Immediately I heard the most delightful sound, like a grand fanfare of celestial silver trumpets. I opened my eyes again in amazement and lay blinking in the morning light; for the night was over! It had passed in a seeming second, and after nearly fifty years this still remains the only experience I have had of this nature. For though I may wake with no memory of dreaming, I still have the feeling that I have been in bed for several hours, and the atmosphere of the unremembered dream still lingers.

Ah me! Great changes have come to pass in the

Seven Sisters Road. The jolly little toy trams have long since gone to the scrap-heap, and the horses that drew them graze in the Elysian fields—at least, I hope they do. The old house, however, still remains, and now and then I pass that way to see once more the windows of the rooms where things "went wrong" so many years ago.

In Finsbury Park itself the change is not so great. The trees we knew still stand and one of the drinking-fountains I was forbidden to use. Sometimes when I sit there I can see, if only in imagination, a very gracious lady whose beauty time shall never dim. She comes across the years to greet me, and all the little golden curls that crowned her brow are radiant in the sun.

CHAPTER II

IT may seem a little surprising, after the events related in the last chapter, that dreams were to have such an absorbing interest for me ; but during my boyhood and youth my health steadily improved, and the nightmare-haunted atmosphere of those early years receded into the past. And now, in my fifties, I am still somewhat delicate, but very hard to kill.

As a schoolboy I was on the whole pretty normal : model steam-engines, air-guns, chemical experiments of a sensational kind, home-made fireworks that exploded prematurely, white mice, stamps, boxing, gymnastics, rowing and cycling—so life passed, pleasantly enough, and on the surface devoid of psychic happenings. I suppose that I was abnormal in three ways, which I will describe very briefly in order to complete my picture of this transitional stage which links the (at the time) incomprehensible happenings of early childhood with the real start of my research.

When I was thirteen I lost my mother, and my father followed her within six months. The Finsbury Park days were over, and I went to live with my grandparents at Southampton. I was too young to realize the irreparable calamity that had befallen me ; but it did at least change my attitude towards death, of which I had been rather afraid till then. Although dying might be a painful business, I felt that beyond the grave I should surely meet my mother, and that thought robbed the mysterious next world of most of its terrors and greatly stimulated my interest in the after-life. Beautiful Mother, big, omniscient Daddy— so short a time before the arbiters of my fate—where were they *now* ? What had happened to them ? I read *Light*, and Stainton Moses. With the aid of a sympathetic school-friend I even dabbled in table-turning and planchette, but the results were neither convincing nor particularly edifying. I soon abandoned these experiments, but continued to read anything on Spiritualism that came my way.

My second abnormality was almost a shameful thing, and clear proof that Fox was really mad ; for I was a poet, and people who should have known better predicted a great future for me. Let me hasten to add that the really remarkable promise of my schoolboy efforts was not fulfilled. The gift matured to some extent ; but later on, when I became increasingly absorbed by my scientific studies, my muse tossed her head and departed. I doubt now whether those early poems were altogether the work of my unaided consciousness. Often there was a preliminary sense of discomfort and restlessness, and I knew I was going to write another "poem". Then all at once the words would seem to form in my brain and I would sense the underlying rhythm. Yes, I incline now to the view that some disembodied poet was trying to get music

out of the very elementary instrument at his or her
disposal. And that is why I have considered the matter
worthy of mention in this record.

My third abnormality has a very direct bearing
upon our subject of astral projection. Though not
indifferent to the charms of Day, her dark sister Night
was dearer far to me. Day's appeal was more a surface
stimulation of the five senses ; but Night pierced deep
and reached perhaps a sixth. I was enthralled by
the moon and the stars and the mystery of that mighty
dome. Sometimes in the winter this longing for Night
would triumph over my love of comfort. In obedience
to her strange call I felt impelled to leave the cosy fire
and my stamps, and ramble over the lonely common
beneath the wondrous stars. And sometimes I would
mount a ladder, reared against the old Roman wall
which bounded one side of our garden, and sit half-
frozen, gazing at the splendid moon. Yes, I loved
Night, and was she not queen of that enchanted place
the Kingdom of Dreams ?

Nightmares were now getting infrequent and
generally of the ordinary kind attributable to an
unwise supper. Glamour and beauty became increasingly manifest in my dream life, and dreams of a new
type came to stimulate my interest. The fortune-
telling side never appealed to me. I glanced through
one popular Dream Book and promptly dismissed it as
bosh, a verdict I still adhere to ; for though a certain
dream may have real prophetic significance for a
certain person, the symbols employed vary according
to the peculiar psychic make-up of the dreamer, and
to attempt to standardize them in the Book-of-Fate

way is absurd. There is no universal language of dreams.

By the time my school-days were over I had reached the following conclusions :

(1) Most of my dreams were obviously a more or less nonsensical mix-up, based on past happenings and memories of books I had read. They might be highly pleasurable and entertaining, but I did not feel that any importance could be attached to them. Here I was, of course, quite wrong ; but Dr. Freud's researches were not to become known to the general public for many years.

(2) Now and then it would happen that a dream possessed real prophetic significance, but only in connection with quite trivial matters. My more mature reflections on this subject, together with some examples, are to be found in "The Prophetic Element in Dreams", published in the *Occult Review* for September, 1920, but here I must restrict myself to this passing reference.

(3) When I dreamed of my mother I did not realize that she was dead, and she did not refer to her passing or tell me anything concerning her new life. Therefore I could not feel sure the dream was not based entirely upon my memories of her. Nevertheless, these dreams were extraordinarily vivid, and so charged with her fragrant atmosphere that on waking it seemed as if I had only just left her presence.

(4) On rare occasions I would have what might be called an historical dream, staged on a really big, spectacular scale and seemingly set in the past. These dreams had two peculiar features : I was not an

actor in them, only a spectator—as though at a vast
open-air theatre ; and I could never remember them
in detail, retaining only a confused impression on
awaking. At first I attributed such dreams to some
dramatizing principle working on my memories of
books and plays, but I wondered why I had not been
cast for an actual part in the drama. Later, however,
when I became acquainted with Theosophy, I favoured
the theory that in these dreams I had contacted the
Akashic Records, or more probably their reflection in
the Astral Light.

If this allusion should be obscure to the general
reader, I must refer him to any elementary text-book
of Theosophy. And here a brief digression is indicated.
Though I am at heart a mystic, I am trying to write
this book more from the standpoint of Psychical
Research, and I shall use Theosophical terms as
sparingly as possible and in no dogmatic spirit. At
times, however, the Theosophical terminology will
prove useful, and it has the great advantage of being
widely known. It is probable that many of my
readers will be Theosophists, and that is why I have
thought it better to speak of "astral" projection and
not "etheric", even though some of my experiences
may perhaps be more etheric in nature, using this
word in the Theosophical sense and without reference
to the postulated ether of Science. According to
Theosophy the etheric double, or etheric body, is a
subtle, interpenetrating extension of the physical
vehicle, and through it circulates the vitalizing life
force. When exteriorized, it cannot move more than a
few feet from its material counterpart, to which it is

attached by a silver cord, and severance of this cord means death. The astral body is a much more subtle vehicle of the consciousness, and though it, too, is linked by another highly complex structure, or cord, to the physical body, it has practically unlimited freedom ; for this cord appears to be of almost infinite elasticity. Now, as sometimes in my out-of-the-body adventures I have *seemed* to travel for many miles, it is obvious that "astral" is the better term for me to use. Thus shall I avoid any confusion with the scientist's "ether", and escape the criticism of my Theosophical friends.

(5) Dreams in which I was exploring what appeared to be a marvellous celestial world exhibiting the most amazing extremes of beauty and ugliness, of attraction and repulsion, of hope and despair. This world was saturated with an indescribable glamour, a seemingly divine atmosphere ; so that, on waking, I felt I had been nearer to God even in a dream-hell than I was in my pleasant room lit by the morning sun.

Dreams of this type were infrequent during my boyhood ; but my youth was rich in them and they engendered a spiritual discontent, which warred against my growing interest in orthodox Science and the gratification of the senses through the ordinary mundane channels. Earth was lovely, but the dream celestial was lovelier still. I was haunted by the memory of a beauty not of this world.

And in these dreams I noted on many occasions what seemed to be the manifestation of some underlying divine law. If the shape of horror was faced boldly it would either be dissipated or actually changed into a thing of beauty, and the latter always happened when my compassion was aroused and conquered my aversion.

(6) I observed that sometimes in a nightmare, or a painful dream of the ordinary non-celestial kind, the very unpleasantness of my predicament would give rise to the thoughts : "But this can't be real ! This wouldn't happen to me ! I must be dreaming !" And then : "I've had enough of this. I'm going to wake up." And I would promptly escape from the situation by, as it were, pushing the dream from me and waking. In those days I never realized the great possibilities latent in this discovery, but my curiosity was aroused to some extent. I wondered why it was only now and then one could get to know *in the dream* that it was a dream, and how was this knowledge acquired ? I think I missed the importance of this experience because I found it was shared by others. It is interesting to note that while many people can escape from a nightmare in this way, very few know they are dreaming if the dream is pleasant or ordinary. It may be that it is the intense emotional *stress* which arouses the critical faculty in the consciousness, enabling it to argue from the extraordinary circumstances of the dream that they are too far removed from everyday life to be real.

Thus in my school-days the forces had been set in motion to urge me through the Gate of Dreams upon my quest, and the time was almost at hand for me to start my great adventure. For it was "great" to me, whatever others may think of it ; and as I am by nature a rather conceited person, why should I affect a modesty I do not really feel ? But I should like to emphasize this point : my sole object in concentrating upon dreams was that I found in some of them a Beauty and Divinity which I most ardently desired but could not find on earth. I knew nothing of astral projection, nor had I the slightest inkling of the surprising turn events would take so soon. I set out in search of Beauty, and in the end I proved, at least to my own satisfaction, that I possessed an immortal soul.

CHAPTER III

In the spring of 1902, when I was midway between my sixteenth and seventeenth birthdays, I started a three years' course in science and electrical engineering at the Hartley Institute, which was later to become the Southampton University College. For me there already existed a sentimental link with the old Hartley : my mother had been a student there in the days before her marriage, and she had often taken me round the museum and discoursed on fossils, while my eyes sought the pickled, double-bodied kitten and the spurious Japanese "mermaids". And it was in the early summer of this year that I had the dream which marks the real beginning of my research.

I dreamed that I was standing on the pavement outside my home. The sun was rising behind the Roman wall, and the waters of Bletchingden Bay were sparkling in the morning light. I could see the tall trees at the corner of the road and the top of the old grey tower beyond the Forty Steps. In the magic of the early sunshine the scene was beautiful enough even then. Now the pavement was not of the ordinary type, but consisted of small, bluish-grey rectangular stones, with their long sides at right-angles to the white kerb. I was about to enter the house when, on glancing casually at these stones, my attention became riveted by a passing strange phenomenon, so extraordinary that I could not believe my eyes—they had seemingly all changed their position in the night, and the long sides were now parallel to the kerb ! Then the solution flashed upon me : though this glorious summer morning seemed as real as real could be, I was *dreaming* !

With the realization of this fact, the quality of the dream changed in a manner very difficult to convey to one who has not had this experience. Instantly the vividness of life increased a hundredfold. Never had sea and sky and trees shone with such glamorous beauty ; even the commonplace houses seemed alive and mystically beautiful. Never had I felt so absolutely well, so clear-brained, so divinely powerful, so inexpressibly *free* ! The sensation was exquisite beyond words ; but it lasted only a few moments, and I awoke. As I was to learn later, my mental control had been overwhelmed by my emotions ; so the tiresome body asserted its claim and pulled me back. For though I did not realize it at the time, I think this first experience was a true projection and that I was actually functioning outside my physical vehicle. Why, when all else was so normal, the position of the paving-stones should have become thus displaced in my consciousness, I cannot explain. These things do happen in the strange astral world which forms the background to such seemingly-objective adventures out of the body, and it is very fortunate for the would-be experimenter that they do. I have always regretted failing to notice whether the stones resumed their proper position before the dream ended.

Although at this time I did not know projection was possible, I was tremendously bucked by my discovery that in a dream one could acquire, by observing some incongruity or anachronism, the knowledge that one was dreaming. The ensuing change in the quality of the dream, and the fact that it did not end immediately, placed this discovery in a very different category from the method of escaping a nightmare mentioned in the previous chapter. Moreover, it led to this exciting question: Was it possible, by the exercise of will-power, to *prolong* the dream ? And I pictured myself, free as air, secure in the consciousness of my true condition and the knowledge that I could always wake if danger threatened, moving like a little god through the glorious scenery of the Dream World.

This new kind of dream I named a Dream of Knowledge ; for one had in it the *knowledge* that one was really dreaming. Before going to sleep I must impress upon my mind the desirability of not allowing the critical faculty to slumber ; it must be kept awake, ready to pounce on any inconsistency in the dream and recognize it as such. It sounds simple ; but in practice I found it one of the most difficult things imaginable. A hundred times would I pass (as I still do) the most glaring incongruities, and then at last some discrepancy would tell me I was dreaming ; and always this knowledge brought, at least to some extent, the change I have described. But I found that though I might know I was dreaming, there were *degrees* of realization, and the vividness or perfection of the experience was proportionate to the extent of the consciousness manifesting in the dream. To get the best results I had to know all about the past life of my earthly self, just as one does in waking life, to realize my body was asleep in bed, and to appreciate the extended powers at my command in this seemingly disembodied state.

In order to attain to the Dream of Knowledge we must arouse the critical faculty which seems to be to a great extent inoperative in dreams, and here, too, degrees of activity become manifest. Let us suppose, for example, that in my dream I am in a café. At a table near mine is a lady who would be very attractive —only, she has four eyes. Here are some illustrations of these degrees of activity of the critical faculty :

(1) In the dream it is practically dormant, but on waking I have the feeling that there was something peculiar about this lady. Suddenly I get it—"Why, of course, she had four eyes !"

(2) In the dream I exhibit mild surprise and say, "How curious, that girl has four eyes ! It spoils her." But only in the same way that I might remark, "What a pity she has broken her nose ! I wonder how she did it."

(3) The critical faculty is more awake and the four eyes are regarded as abnormal ; but the phenomenon is not fully appreciated. I exclaim, "Good Lord !" and then reassure myself by adding, "There must be a freak show or a circus in the town." Thus I hover on the brink of realization, but do not quite get there.

(4) My critical faculty is now fully awake and refuses to be satisfied by this explanation. I continue

my train of thought, "But there never was such a freak! An adult woman with four eyes—it's *impossible*. I am dreaming."

I hope I have not laboured this point ; but I have found to my surprise that some people are quite unable to grasp this idea of the Dream of Knowledge, that it is really a new level of consciousness and different from the states experienced in ordinary dreams and in waking life. They object, "But after all, it's only a dream. How can a dream be anything else ?" And their expression is eloquent of the doubt they are too polite to voice.

Well, to resume, I found that in these Dreams of Knowledge new methods of locomotion were open to me. I could glide along the surface of the ground, passing through seemingly solid walls, etc., at a great speed, or I could levitate to a height of about one hundred feet and then glide. I shall return to these methods later on. I could also do some intriguing little tricks at will, such as moving objects without visible contact, and moulding the plastic matter into new forms ; but in these early experiments I could stay out of my body for only a very short time, and this special dream-consciousness could be acquired only at intervals of several weeks. To begin with, my progress was very slow ; but presently I made two more discoveries :

(1) The mental effort of prolonging the dream produced a pain in the head—dull at first, but rapidly increasing in intensity—and I knew instinctively this was a warning to me to resist no longer the call of my body.

(2) In the last moments of prolonging the dream, and while I was subject to this pain, I experienced a most curious sensation, as of dual consciousness. I could feel myself standing in the dream and see the scenery; but at the same time I could feel myself lying in bed and see my bedroom. As the call of the body grew stronger the dream-scenery became more faint; but by asserting my will to remain dreaming I could make the bedroom fade and the dream-scenery regain its apparent solidity.

And at this stage of my research a new query arose : what would happen if I disregarded the warning pain and fought it to a climax ? As a matter of fact I was horribly afraid of making the experiment, but a sense of destiny urged me on. About a year after the paving-stones dream I screwed up my courage, took the risk, won the battle, and had a never-to-be-forgotten adventure.

I dreamed that I was walking by the water on the Western Shore. It was morning ; the sky a light blue ; the foam-flecked waves were greenish in the sunshine. I forget just how it happened, but something told me that I was dreaming. Perhaps I walked through a telegraph-post, or became aware that my body had no weight. I decided to prolong the dream and continued my walk, the scenery now appearing extraordinarily vivid and clear. Very soon my body began to draw me back. I experienced dual consciousness : I could feel myself lying in bed and walking by the sea at one and the same time. Moreover, I could dimly see the objects in my bedroom, as well as the dream-scenery. I willed to continue dreaming. A battle ensued ; now my bedroom became clearly visible and the shore-scene dim ; then my bedroom would become indistinct and the shore-scene brighter. My will triumphed. I lost the sense of dual consciousness. My bedroom faded altogether from my vision, and I was out on the shore, feeling indescribably free and elated. Soon my body began to call again, and at the same time I became aware of a sharp, neuralgic pain in my forehead (not my physical forehead) and the top of my head. As I willed to continue dreaming, this pain increased in intensity ; but this time there was no dual conscious-ness, or alternating clearness of bedroom and shore—the bedroom was not visible. I fought against my body by steadily willing to remain in the Dream World. The pain in my forehead gradually increased, reached a maximum, and then, to my delight, suddenly ceased. As the pain vanished, something seemed to "click" in my brain. I had won the battle. My body pulled no longer, and I was free.

I continued my walk, revelling in the beauty of the morning and my sense of freedom. I encountered no one, which was not surprising, for few people passed that way early in the day. How long elapsed I cannot say ; time is a most perplexing thing in the Dream World ; but presently it occurred to me that I ought to be getting back to my body. I had to be at College by nine o'clock, and I had no idea what the actual earth-time was, except that it was probably morning. I therefore willed to end the dream and to awake. To my great surprise nothing happened. It was as though a man actually wide awake willed to awake. It seemed to me that I could not be more awake than I was. My reason told me that the apparently solid shore and sunlit waves were not the physical land and sea; that my body was lying in bed, half a mile away at Forest View; but I could not feel the *truth* of this. I seemed to be completely severed from that physical body. At this point I became aware of a man and a boy approaching. As they passed me they were talking together; they did not seem to see me, but I was not quite sure. A little later, however, when I met another man and asked him the time, he took no notice and was evidently unaware of my presence. And then I wondered if I was "dead". Worse still, if I was in danger of suffering premature burial! What was the real time—the actual time on earth? How long had this dream lasted?

I began to feel terribly lonely. This experience was quite new to me: always before I had been able to wake when I cared to will it—indeed, the trouble had been that I woke too easily. Now I was afraid, and it was difficult to keep control and not give way to panic. Desperately I willed to wake—again and again, until a climax was reached. Something seemed to snap. Again I had that queer sensation of a "click" within my brain. I was awake now—yes, but completely paralysed! I could not open my eyes. I could not speak. I could not move a muscle. I had a slight sense of daylight shining through my eyelids, and I could distinctly hear the clock ticking and my grandfather moving about in the adjoining room.

Now, although my position was sufficiently unpleasant, I did not feel as frightened as I had when out of my body. It seemed to me imperative that I should remain as calm as possible. To this end I mentally repeated the Binomial Theorem and several other mathematical formulæ. I then concentrated on willing to move my body as a whole. The result was an absolute failure. I was feeling more frightened now, but I managed to keep fairly calm. Then I had an inspiration : I would devote all my mental energy to raising just my little finger. I succeeded. The third and middle fingers followed. I then was able to move my whole hand—the right one. Then I managed to raise my arm above my head and to grip the bed-rail. I was still blind, and the rest of my body seemed made of iron. Willing steadily to rise, I tugged and tugged at the bed-rail. At first without success, and then quite suddenly the trance was broken. In an instant my eyes were open to the light, and my body was sitting up. Joyfully I sprang out of bed, then staggered and had to lean against the post. For a few moments I was a prey to deathly sickness and feared that I would faint, but I speedily recovered. It was eight o'clock, so I had to hurry to get to College in time. I felt rather unwell and very depressed for the rest of the day, though not seriously inconvenienced. About three days passed before I regained my normal health and spirits.

This was my first experience of that deep trance state in which the physical body appears to the experimenter to be in a cataleptic condition. The way in which this was overcome (by raising first the little finger, etc.) may have been an illusion, i.e. there may have been no movements of the physical body before the trance was broken—though the fact that I found myself sitting up is in favour of the physical reality of the means whereby the trance was ended. No proof is possible one way or the other in this case, as no one but the experimenter was there to observe what actually happened.

For a time this fright had a sobering effect, and then the rashness of youth broke out once more ; yet perhaps it was the urge of the investigator, and not the adventurous mystic in me, which made me repeat my experiment of ignoring the call of the body. Allowance must be made for my age, but I thought I had stumbled upon something really big and I wanted to confirm my results.

Through prolonging a dream (the details of which were not remembered) in defiance of the warning pain, I again experienced great difficulty in leaving the dream and awaking. Again I found myself in a state resembling catalepsy and had to resort to the methods already described. This time, however, when I had succeeded in raising one arm the trance was broken· I experienced slight sickness and felt the effects, fatigue and depression, for the rest of the day. An unusual feature was that all memory of the details of the dream was lost in the stress of breaking the trance.

This experience was certainly less severe than the first recorded, but it was sufficiently unpleasant to deter me for several years from running the risk of another. I had experienced this cataleptic trance twice within a few weeks, and felt that I was "playing with fire". I feared heart-failure, premature burial, or the possibility of becoming obsessed. And, of course, I was in love and life seemed sweet. So for many months, in my further experiments in prolonging dreams, I always took the pain in my forehead to be a direct warning to return to my body. When I felt it, I willed to break from the dream, and I had no difficulty in waking.

Catalepsy can be produced by hypnosis, and it is very probable that my symptoms were actually physical and not merely an illusion of the trance state; but I know now there was no need for me to have had that painful struggle to break the condition. If I had just composed my mind and dozed off again, my body would have been normal on waking. I have proved this on many occasions, and can recommend it as much the better course to pursue if any reader should find himself, perhaps quite by accident, in this state; for the mental strain and tendency to panic might react unfavourably upon a weak heart.

My fear of premature burial was also groundless; for as I had not received medical attention for a year or so, a post-mortem would have been necessary, and the trance would most probably have been dispelled by the surgeon's knife before the body had suffered much damage. There might, however, be a very serious risk of premature burial in cases where an inquest would not follow, if the cataleptic condition proved to be of exceptional severity.

CHAPTER IV

THE FALSE AWAKENING AND THE TRANCE CONDITION

I SIGH for the days when I was young and a student at the dear old Hartley. Wonderful days! How quickly the three years passed! My interests were so many and varied; in that magical period of my youth even this commonplace old world of ours seemed glamorous and full of the promise of adventure; and— smile if it please you—always at the back of my mind was the delightful thought, kept more or less a secret, that I was really *different* from other men. I was a sort of celestial pioneer, an explorer of the vast, unseen, transcendent realm of Spirit, and destined, it might be, to make some great discovery for the lasting benefit of mankind.

Yet must it be recorded that this pioneer wasted his rarely-found opportunities for research very badly. It was so difficult to maintain the role of an impersonal observer in this strange Dream World, to realize that if I allowed my emotions to get the better of my mental control the dream would come to an abrupt end. I would enter a restaurant and order a meal, only to wake after savouring the first few mouthfuls. Indeed, to see how much one could eat, without paying attention to the taste, would form a very good exercise in mental control if only these Dreams of Knowledge were more easily come by; but, as things are, there are better ways of spending one's time in the dream, and I do not recommend it. Similarly I would visit a theatre, but could never stay in the dream more than a few minutes after the curtain had risen, because my growing interest in the play broke down my mental control of the experience. I would encounter a fascinating lady and even talk to her for a little while, but the mere thought of a possible embrace was fatal. Of course, I found a ready excuse for my repeated failures ; I was just getting experience in control. I was very slow to learn that the motto for the pro- jectionist should be : "I may look, but I must not get too interested—let alone touch !"

A fellow student named Barrow, whose father was a Theosophist, brought the subject of Theosophy actively to my notice ; but before this I had come across re- ferences to it in *Light* in connection with reincarnation. I read several of the elementary manuals and was much impressed by the resemblance between my "celestial dreams" and the astral plane of Theosophy. Also, Annie Besant paid a visit to Southampton, lecturing at the Philharmonic Hall, and I soon succumbed to the charm of her oratory. But though I found a wealth of new and fascinating ideas in my Theosophical studies, I could not find anything of practical use to me in my dream-research, nor could I find any mention of this peculiar dream in which one has the knowledge of dreaming. I rather think it was hinted that Masters and very high Adepts were able to leave their bodies at will, but no information was vouchsafed concerning their methods, nor was one encouraged to suppose that such a thing was possible for ordinary people.

One day Barrow said to me, "Do you believe in Astrology ?"

"No," I replied, "it's all rot. An exploded science."

"How do you know it is ?" he persisted. "Have you ever read a book on it ? Can you cast a horoscope ?"

"No, but the scientific johnnies say there's nothing in it," I protested somewhat feebly.

"Yes, because they're too narrow-minded to investigate. They'd say just the same about Theosophy or your blessed old dream-research."

Which decided me to look into it for myself. So we made acquaintance with the works of Raphael, Zadkiel, Sepharial, and benevolent bright-eyed Alan Leo—the "big" little man who stood head and shoulders above the rest. And we found that Astrology *did* work, though *why* it should was beyond our comprehension. But when all our knowledge is relative, it is foolish to trouble over-much about the "whys". Thus a new interest came into my life and has lasted even unto this day.

Before leaving this subject I would add, for the information of any astrological reader, that I was born at 9.10 a.m., November 30, 1885, at Southampton. My projection experiences are perhaps indicated by the double-bodied sign Sagittarius rising with the Sun therein. Also a loose triple-conjunction of Jupiter, Herschel and the Moon occupies the Ninth House—the house of religion, philosophy, science and long journeys —and the Moon in Virgo is in close trine with Neptune, planet of trance, in the Fifth.

Two isolated experiments may be noted here :

On the eve of sitting for an examination in machine

construction, I willed to dream of seeing the paper that would be set.   I dreamed that I was taking the examination, and, knowing that I was dreaming, attempted to memorize the questions upon the paper.   On awakening, I remembered two : (1) Sketch and describe some form of steam-separator. (2) Sketch a grease-box suitable for a goods-truck.   The next day, when I actually took the examination, I found both these questions upon the paper.   They did not appear as complete questions by themselves, but were sections of others.   The first was a likely question ; but a persual of past papers (made *after* the dream) showed that the second question had not been asked for many years. I might have brought through more details of the paper but for the fact that in a Dream of Knowledge reading is a very difficult matter.   The print seems clear enough until one tries to read it ; then the letters become blurred, or run together, or fade away, or change to others.

Each line, or in some cases each word, must be held by an effort of the will until its meaning has been grasped ; then it is released—on which it becomes blotted out or changed—and the next held in its turn and so on.   Other people have told me that they find the same difficulty in reading dream-literature ; but I have not as yet seen any really satisfactory theory to account for it.   It is highly improbable that I could have repeated this success, but I did not try ; for after the experiment I had an uneasy feeling that it was not quite playing the game.   It was true other people were at liberty to do the same thing, but I knew it would never occur to them to make the attempt.

The other experiment was as follows :

I had been spending the evening with two friends, Slade and Elkington, and our conversation had turned to the subject of dreams. Before parting, we agreed to meet, if possible, on Southampton Common in our dreams that night. I dreamed I met Elkington on the Common as arranged, but Slade was not present. We both knew we were dreaming and commented on Slade's absence. After which the dream ended, being of very short duration. The next day when I saw Elkington I said nothing at first of my experience, but asked him if he had dreamed. "Yes," he replied, "I met you on the Common all right and knew I was dreaming, but old Slade didn't turn up. We had just time to greet each other and comment on his absence, then the dream ended." On interviewing Slade we learned that he had not dreamed at all, which perhaps accounted for his inability to keep the appointment.

Some people have raised the objection, "Oh, well, you expected to meet your friend and so you dreamed you did. That's all." But if expectation is to explain the experience, then I expected to meet Elkington and *Slade*, while Elkington expected to meet *Slade* and me. How is it, then, expectation failed us both with regard to Slade ? Why was he absent ? How is it expectation failed to make him dream of meeting us ? Elkington and I were unable to repeat this small success. The whole question bristles with difficulties ; but I believe it is an extremely rare occurrence for two people to share apparently the same dream-experience and for *both* to remember it on awaking.

My next discoveries were the False Awakening and

the Trance Condition—the latter being really a much milder form of the cataleptic state already described and merging into it if the trance grows deeper, as later experience was to show.   Sometimes after a Dream of Knowledge, and less frequently after an unremembered dream, I would seem to wake and remain quite under the impression that I was awake, and then some abnormal happening would show me I was in a state of trance.

I will now give three examples from my records :

(1) I passed from unremembered dreams and thought I was awake.   It was still night, and my room very dark.   Although it seemed to me that I was awake, I felt curiously disinclined to move.   The atmosphere seemed changed, to be in a "strained" condition.   I had a sense of invisible, intangible powers at work, which caused this feeling as of aerial stress.   I became expectant.   Certainly something was about to happen. Suddenly the room was faintly illuminated.   A soft greenish glow, suggesting phosphorescence, was emanating from a glass-doored Japanese cabinet beside my bed.   From this source it spread slowly and evenly, like a luminous gas—a cold, spectral light, of unvarying brightness.   For a while I stayed motionless, watching it.   I did not feel afraid, but I was filled with wonder. Then, wishing to observe more closely the source of this mysterious light, I made an effort to overcome my strange disinclination to move.   Instantly the light vanished and things were as usual.   I was really awake now, with my head half raised from the pillow.

Note : I did not know it, but I could have left my body quite easily (by the method of instantaneous projection) when in this condition, as will become apparent later on. The glow, though real enough on its own plane, was from the physical standpoint only an illusion.

(2) My friend Barrow had arranged with me that he would attempt to precipitate his astral vehicle, while asleep, and appear to me in my bedroom. My experience was as follows :

I dreamed of being in the main hall of the Hartley University College, and there I met my mother. This meeting did not surprise me ; for I knew quite well that I was dreaming—though *how* I knew, I cannot say. I told her I was expecting an astral visit from Barrow and must go back to my bedroom and await his coming. Instantly I was caught up, as though in some invisible current, and borne back to my body. I awoke— at least, I was certainly under the impression that I was awake—and was much annoyed by this abrupt termination to the experiment.

"If only I had managed to stay in the dream," I thought, "I could have waited here (in the astral counterpart of my bedroom) and have met him if he came ; but now, even if he does come, as I am awake I shall not be able to see him, for I am not clairvoyant.

At this point I became aware of two things : (1) That a sudden almost indescribable change had been effected in the atmosphere, which seemed charged with expectation (the "before a storm" sensation intensified) and rarefied, or perhaps compressed. It seemed to me that the atmosphere was being strained by the working of some unknown force. (2) That my bedroom door, which had been shut, was now ajar—a faint golden light streaming through the opening.

I had just time to note these things and then, literally in a flash, my friend came. He did not enter by the door. He appeared instantaneously, in an egg-shaped cloud of intense bluish-white light, and stood by my bed, gravely regarding me. He was dressed in a white robe (possibly his nightshirt) ; and as my eyes recovered from the dazzling effect of his sudden appearance, I saw that inside the bluish-white ovoid surrounding him were bands of colour—deep red, rose-red, violet, blue, sea-green and pale orange. Excepting the last-mentioned, I cannot remember the order in which they were arranged ; but the pale orange was centred around the head, shooting upwards from it in a widening conical ray until it reached the ceiling. As I lay there (on the left side of my double-bed) watching him, I felt paralysed—not with fear, but astonishment and admiration. He did not speak, but I felt that he was telling me mentally not to be afraid. It must be remembered that all this happened in a moment or two ; then, even as I struggled to break the strange inertia possessing me and to address him, he vanished as suddenly as he had come.

Again, seemingly wide awake, I lay in the darkness ; but before my surprise at his abrupt disappearance had faded, a fresh phenomenon arrested my attention. In the air above the foot of my bed appeared a circle of yellow light, as though projected from a magic-lantern, and in this were three figures—a man and two women— enacting a drama of the "eternal triangle" description. These figures were about three feet high ; the dress was modern, and the colouring perfect ; but I cannot remember what the background was like. I could not actually hear their words, but I knew mentally what was being said. This play seemed to last several minutes, and considerations of space forbid more detailed reference. It ended for me when one woman stabbed the other. Mentally I heard the victim's scream, and the induced shock terminated the trance. The scene vanished instantly, and I lay, really awake now, staring into the darkness.

Note : Barrow's dream-experience proved disappointing. He had no recollection of having been in my room, but he did remember that he had found himself at the foot of the Forty Steps—only two minutes' walk from my home. He had also several other dreams, but no memory of these remained. We had originally decided to meet (in our dreams) in the hall of the Hartley, but abandoned this idea in favour of my friend's attempt at astral projection. In the first stage of my dream I was evidently adhering to our original plan, and I have little doubt that this was an actual projection on my part.

From the scientific standpoint, the door ajar, Barrow's apparition and the play may all be regarded as illusions experienced in the Trance Condition—that is, these phenomena had no existence on the physical plane of waking life. From the occult standpoint, however, Barrow's apparition, encased in the auric egg, may have been an actual fact, as real on its plane of manifestation as any physical phenomenon is on earth. Occultists will agree that the absence of recollection on his part does not affect the genuineness of the projection, while the presence of the well-marked aura supports this and is in opposition to the theory that I saw merely a thought-form of my own making. In those days my idea of the aura was very vague and I certainly should not have imagined him in the form in which he appeared.

It may be remarked that Barrow was an intellectual person, probably a highly evolved soul, and that yellow is the colour denoting the Manasic element—the mentality. Nevertheless, though it may be just jealousy on my part, this aura does seem to have been a bit too splendid—more what one would expect to find with an Adept. And now, in the interests of science, I must suggest another more probable, but rather unkind, theory : that what I saw was not Barrow's astral vehicle, but a thought-form emanating from *him* ; for at that time he was ahead of me in Theosophical matters and was well acquainted with pictures of the aura. It must be understood, of course, that even if this theory be true it does not involve any conscious deception on his part.

The play may have been the creation of one part of my consciousness, being objectified in the process, so that it seemed an external thing to the part observing the phenomenon. Again, it may have been an astral play, or even a fragment from the Records reflected in the Astral Light. I do not know. Mention has been made of a similar bright circle in Chapter I.

(3) I passed from an unremembered dream to find myself apparently awake in the darkness of my room. In a moment or two I became aware of that curious change in the atmosphere which has already been

described. The thought came to me that something unusual was about to happen, but I had no idea as to the form this expected manifestation would take. Then, with startling suddenness, an ovoid of bluish-white appeared a few feet from my bed, and in it was a seemingly solid figure which I instantly recognized. The apparition was clothed in a simple white robe of intense brilliance, but no astral colours were discernible. The face was on the lines of the orthodox representations of Christ and wondrously beautiful. I think the hair and beard were a dark shade of reddish-brown, and the eyes were a deep dark blue. The expression was orthodox too, being mild and sorrowful. I must admit that I was awed by this vision, and its very beauty seemed to increase the paralysis afflicting me. After some fraction of time I succeeded in overcoming this inability to move. I stretched out a hand to touch the figure, and then it immediately vanished. Not a word had been spoken. I was now awake and found my body, supported on one elbow, half-raised from the bed ; my left arm was still outstretched.

Note : I have pleaded guilty to being rather a conceited person, but even in those days I was not conceited enough to believe this experience was really what it appeared to be. It has been suggested to me that some Adept, who happened to pass my way, noted my entranced condition and assumed this shape in order to quicken the devotional element within me. If this be the true explanation, I cannot understand why the Adept did not choose a less conventional form. Much compulsory church-going and "religious instruction" had successfully nipped in the bud any interest I might have felt in Christianity. The popular conception of Christ appealed to the poet in me, but it did not stir my religious instincts—perhaps because it was too familiar. Had the form taken been Indian, or even Chinese, I should have been much more impressed and more ready to believe that this apparition was really a celestial visitor of high grade. Taking into consideration the absence of the auric colours, which one would most certainly expect to see, I think this figure was only a thought form, though of exceptional beauty and power, emanating from some unknown source. Nevertheless, it was a noteworthy experience and unforgettable.

The house, which was my home at this period of my life, seemed to be haunted by an earth-bound spirit. Often in the night, or even in the light of early morning, I would hear footsteps ascending and descending the stairs, and sometimes they had a nasty trick of stopping just outside my door—and this when I was really awake and not in the Trance Condition. I funked several opportunities and then one night, when the "ghost" paused in this way, I bounded out of bed and had the door wide open in a trice. I could not see anything, and I readily admit I was more relieved than disappointed as I turned in again.

On one occasion my grandfather and I heard these footsteps together. We were alone in the house, for our housekeeper had provided us with a cold supper and gone out to visit a friend. So we sat by the fire, reading in silence. Then we distinctly heard footsteps descending the stairs and passing along the passage to the kitchen. My grandfather looked up from his book in mild surprise.

"Why, I did not know Emma had come back," he exclaimed. "Did you ? She's early tonight."

"No, I never heard her come in," I replied indifferently ; for the sounds were so real that he merely seemed to be stating an indisputable fact.

But about twenty minutes later we regarded each other in mute astonishment as a key turned in the front door. It was Emma, and we had been alone in the house when we heard the footsteps. The back door was bolted, just as she had left it when she went out.

Sometimes, when the footsteps halted outside my bedroom, I would hear a sound as though the door-knob were being turned, which added to the eerie nature of the proceedings ; but as this invariably happened in the darkness, I could not tell if the knob actually moved. I was able to eliminate our cat from the problem ; for, as I was first down in the morning, I could confirm that he was still locked up in the kitchen. I tried balancing a button on the knob, so that the slightest audible movement would cause it to fall ; but curiously enough every time I did this, even though I might hear the steps, I did not hear the knob turned and the button was still balanced in the morning. So I never solved the mystery.

CHAPTER V

THE ELSIE PROJECTION

In the summer of 1905 I had a sweetheart whom I will call "Elsie". Our ways in life were fated to diverge and for many years I have had no news of her. But if Elsie has not made the last projection and should chance to read these lines, she will know that I have not forgotten her. And really, there is no need for me to add how happy I should be to hear from her again.

Well, Elsie viewed my experimenting with extreme disfavour. It was wicked, she felt, and God would be seriously angry with me if I persisted. Anyhow, *she* didn't like it, and that was that!

Then I, with all the painful seriousness of youth, kindly explained to her that she was only a narrow-minded little ignoramus and did not know what she was talking about. Did she even know the meaning of astral projection?

"Yes," said Elsie with great emphasis, "I do! I know more than you think. I could go to you tonight if I wanted to."

Whereat I laughed rudely and immoderately; for she knew no more of occultism, theoretical or practical, than I of needlework. Elsie, small blame to her, lost her temper.

"Very well," she exclaimed, "I'll *prove* it ! It's wicked, but I don't care. I'll come to your room to-night and you shall see me there."

"All right," I replied, not in the least impressed, "come if you can."

Then we ended our quarrel and presently I walked home—over a mile from Elsie's—and straightway forgot her in reading for my exams. I went to bed late and very tired. Her boast had seemed so childish that I never gave it a thought.

Some time in the night, while it was still dark, I woke—but it was the False Awakening. I could hear the clock ticking and dimly see the objects in the room. I lay on the left side of my double-bed, with tingling nerves, waiting. Something was going to happen. But what ? Even then I did not think of Elsie.

Suddenly there appeared a large egg-shaped cloud of intensely brilliant bluish-white light. In the middle was Elsie, hair loose, and in her nightdress. She seemed perfectly solid as she stood by a chest of drawers near the right side of my bed. Thus she remained, regarding me with calm but sorrowful eyes, and running her fingers along the top and front side of a desk which stood on the drawers. She did not speak.

For what seemed to be some seconds I could not move or utter a word. Again I felt the strange paralysis which I have previously noted. Wonder and admiration filled me, but I was not afraid of her. At last I broke the spell. Rising on one elbow I called her name, and she vanished as suddenly as she had come. It certainly seemed I was awake now.

"I must note the time," I thought, but an irresistible

drowsiness overwhelmed me. I fell back and slept dreamlessly till morning.

The following evening we met and I found Elsie very excited and triumphant.

"I did come to you!" she greeted me. "I *really* did. I went to sleep, willing that I would, and all at once I was *there*! This morning I knew just how everything was in your room, but I've been forgetting all day—it's been slipping away."

Oh, that unscientific mind of hers! Why didn't she make notes? Well, despite her impatience, I would not say a word about what I had seen until she had told me all she could remember. So, although this experience can never be absolutely convincing to her or to anyone else, it is at least to me.

She described in detail the following :

(1) Relative positions of door, bed, window, fireplace, washstand, chest of drawers and dressing-table.

(2) That the window had a number of small panes instead of the more usual large ones.

(3) That I was lying, eyes open, on the left side of a double-bed (I had never told her it was double) and seemed dazed.

(4) An old-fashioned pin-cushion, an unusual object in a man's room.

(5) A black Japanese box covered with red raised figures.

(6) A leather-covered desk lined with gilt, sunk plate on top for handle to fall back into, standing on the chest of drawers. She described how she was running her fingers along a projecting ridge on the front of this desk.

"You're wrong in just one thing," I said later. "What you took for a ridge was a gilt line on the leather. There's no projecting ridge anywhere."

"There is," said Elsie positively, "I tell you I *felt* it."

"But, my dear girl," I protested, "don't you think I know my own desk ?"

"I don't care !" she replied. "When you go home look at it, and you will find a gilt ridge on the front side."

I took her advice. The desk was placed to front the wall, and the hinges (which I had quite forgotten) made a continuous projecting gilt ridge just as she had described. Owing to its position, she had naturally mistaken the back of the desk for the front. Though elated by her success, she still maintained that such experiments were "wicked" and I could never persuade her to come to me again.

I am positive that Elsie, in the flesh, had never seen my room ; for, as she never visited my home, she could not have had a peep without my knowledge, nor could she have obtained a description from any common friend. I am also quite sure that I had never told her about the pin-cushion, Japanese box and desk. Perhaps I had better say here that an account of this projection was published anonymously in the *Weekly Tale-Teller* for July 11, 1914.

Elsie's statement that my eyes were *open* raises an interesting question : were they really open, or did they only seem so to her ? My physical eyes were certainly shut in my cataleptic experiences, for then I was blind, except for the light penetrating my eyelids. In the other trance happenings I have described it seemed to me that my eyes were open ; but for reasons to be explained later, I now think my physical eyes were closed. They actually opened at the moment the trance was broken, so that I found myself staring into the darkness. Elsie probably saw the open eyes of my astral, or perhaps my etheric, counterpart.

I have never ceased being grateful to dear Elsie for being "wicked" just for once. Truth to tell, though a few of my friends were sympathetic, the world refused to be impressed by my great discovery, or even to take it seriously. When I tried to get into print, one editor actually insinuated in polite-nasty fashion that mouse-like flying quadrupeds inhabited my campanile. Therefore in the years to come I had my periods of reaction and downright scepticism. After all, *was* there anything in my research ? Might not my out-of-the-body adventures be purely subjective—just imagination or dream-stuff ? But always when I pondered on the Elsie projection my spirits rose. I *had* discovered something of great importance, but the time was not yet ripe to give it to the world. I knew—and indeed I still know—that Elsie was in my room that night in her spirit, though her body was in bed a mile away. Elsie had a soul or spirit, and that meant I had one, and if I really had a soul—well, then my soul was *not* in my body when I was "locked out" on the shore. And if the soul could leave the body while the latter still lived, was there not every reason to suppose man had an immortal spirit ? Perhaps no rigid proof was possible, but it made the whole thing—this question of immortality and the soul and God—so much more probable. Yes, I must keep on. O thrice-blessed Elsie! You never knew how much you did for me that night.

In this same summer of 1905, all unwittingly, I gave Elsie quite a nasty fright. She woke on a bright morning to find me standing, fully dressed but hatless, by her bed. I looked so solid and real that she never doubted I was there in the flesh. She slept with her window wide open, and she thought I had been emulating Romeo and had chosen a singularly inappropriate time. She could hear her brother whistling merrily in the next room and her mother coming up the stairs to hers, to see if she was getting up, as was her custom. Poor Elsie was in a terrible state. She wanted so desperately to warn me that discovery was only a matter of seconds, but she seemed paralysed and could not move or speak. I just stood there, solid and stolid, very serious and silent. Then, as the door-knob turned, I vanished and her mother entered. I am sure Elsie gave me a truthful account of how things seemed to her, but she was clearly in the Trance Condition. I verified that I was asleep at the time, but I had no memory of the happening.

Sometimes after the False Awakening I had the rather frightening experience of feeling an apparently solid hand touching or gripping me. As I lay in the darkness I would satisfy myself as to the position of my own hands—that they were underneath the clothes— yet a *third* hand would be pressing on my forehead. On one occasion I was seized by steel-like arms and squeezed until I seemed to be gasping for breath. At last I managed to cry out, and as the trance was broken I saw a misty white shape dissolving in the night. One apparition of a non-human kind particularly impressed me ; indeed, the intrepid pioneer gave a yell that broke the trance very effectively. My visitor resembled a conical mass of glistening snow and nearly reached the ceiling. It had no features, but two blazing blue eyes completed the picture. After I had got over my scare, I came to the conclusion that this strange shape was not malevolent in nature and probably had a real existence on its plane of manifestation. I now think it belonged to the Deva Kingdom, but the reader is quite welcome to consider it merely as an illusion experienced in the Trance Condition.

I heard also, when in this state, in addition to physical sounds, several strange noises: crackling sounds suggesting electrical phenomena ; roaring and whirring noises as of gigantic machines ; a peculiar snapping sound, recalling the driving-bands, used to transmit power in a workshop ; sounds like the surging of an angry sea and rushing winds ; and sometimes voices calling. Some of these sounds may have been caused by variations in blood-pressure, but I do not think that all of them can be accounted for in this way.

By the end of my College days the results of my research can be briefly summarized as follows :

(1) The Dream of Knowledge and the peculiar powers enjoyed therein.

(2) Dual Consciousness.

(3) The Warning Pain.

(4) The Cataleptic State.

(5) The False Awakening.

(6) The Trance Condition and the apparitions, sounds and other phenomena associated therewith.

And so farewell to Forest View and that house near the Roman wall. Southampton has changed almost out of recognition. The Western Shore is now a stretch of factories and huge docks ; but the old grey tower still stands a time-worn sentinel beside the Forty Steps, while in the distance the graceful mighty shape of the *Queen Mary* slowly passes by. Only on the screen of the Eternal Records shall the waters of Bletchingden Bay still sparkle in the sunshine ; and there a sentimental youngster, locked out in his dream, still wanders by them.

CHAPTER VI

DREAM OF KNOWLEDGE NOT ESSENTIAL :
ANOTHER METHOD

WHEN I planned this book, I decided to confine myself to the subject of Astral Projection and to make only passing reference, where necessary, to my investigations in other branches of occultism. It seemed desirable also to exclude all autobiographical matter that had little direct bearing on my subject. Nevertheless, if only to explain why my progress was so slow, a very brief account of my rolling-stone activities is, I think, permissible, and it will provide some sort of background to this record.

By the time my three years' course was over, I had come to the conclusion that I did not like the practical dirty-overalls side of engineering, but that I was very keen on laboratory research-work. What seemed a certain job on these lines fell through at the last moment and no other was forthcoming. So, much to the sorrow of my grandfather, I packed the whole thing up and joined a tenth-rate theatrical company, which was great fun. I did a little research-work too—on the variations in consciousness resulting from the absorption of different kinds of alcoholic beverages. When I came of age I found myself with nearly £300, the remnant of a legacy which would have been quite comfortable if things like the Liberator smash had never happened. However, it seemed a fortune to me ; so I abandoned the Thespian Art and promptly took unto myself a wife—perhaps the wisest thing I have ever done. There followed two unsuccessful business ventures and then I decided I would be an author. And eventually I was—of a sort—and led a delightfully lazy, but very precarious, existence as a writer of magazine stories until the cataclysm of the Great War.

It will now be evident why my enthusiasm for my dream-research waned almost to extinction in the first few years after I left the Hartley. It is true I continued to have experiences of the Dream of Knowledge and made some projections ; but I never troubled to record them, and now they have completely vanished from my mind. I do not know why, but the impression made on the brain by these out-of-the-body adventures is extremely fugitive. They should be noted in detail as soon as possible after the event— which is a great nuisance as it breaks the night's rest. I have certainly not been the ideal investigator : I have been lazy and have worked only by fits and starts, pulled this way and that by conflicting ambitions and other interests. Two of my early note-books have vanished and were probably destroyed in the clear-up preceding a move. I still have notes of several hundred dreams, but of these only about sixty can rank as true projections. I have, however, made many more which were either never recorded or in the lost books.

I find a brief note, made in August, 1906, of another apparition seen in the Trance Condition. This time it was of the lady who was shortly to become my wife. She was at Southampton, and I in West Kensington. I passed from a forgotten dream to find myself apparently awake ; disinclination to move and the atmospheric changes previously described. The apparition was similar to Elsie's and vanished on my moving, which broke the trance. No words were spoken and no astral colours were visible. My wife-to-be was asleep at the time, but had no memory of dreaming.

Then a gap occurs in my records until July, 1908, and this experience marks a really big advance :

Lying on the sofa in the afternoon with my eyes closed, I suddenly found that I could see the pattern on the sofa-back. This told me that I was in the Trance Condition. I then left my body, by willing myself out of it, and experienced an extremely sudden transition to a beautiful unknown stretch of country. There I walked for some time over wild and charming ground beneath a bright blue sky in which were fleecy sunlit clouds. All too soon my body called me back, and on my homeward flight I distinctly remember passing right through a horse and van which were standing in some unfamiliar street. The actual appearance of the London sky at the time of making this experiment is unknown to me. I should have made a point of observing it directly the trance was over.

The importance of this entry lies in two things :

(1) It showed that the Dream of Knowledge, which I had hitherto regarded as an indispensable preliminary to projection, was not really essential and could be dispensed with altogether. For I had not actually been to sleep, but was only in a drowsy condition, when I dis-

covered that I could see through my closed eyes. It was as though I had an inner pair which had suddenly opened. This meant that, when conditions were favourable, it was possible to pass into the Trance Condition without the intervening dream and that one could experiment at *any time* and not only on the rare occasions when the critical faculty had been kept awake in the dream. I was to find, however, that both methods were equally difficult; for, though the initial stages of the trance were easily induced, the very slightest disturbance was sufficient to break the condition before it had become sufficiently deep to allow of separation.

(2) Ridiculous as it may appear to the reader, I had never realized that the Trance Condition *preceded* the act of projection. Probably because of my two early cataleptic experiences, I thought the order of the phenomena was : Dream of Knowledge, Projection, False Awakening, and then the Trance Condition as the concluding phase. Yes, now it seems very stupid of me ; but it must be remembered that I was working quite alone and that there was no literature on the subject available in those days. It was just an inspiration which made me attempt to leave my body on this occasion, a thing I had never thought of doing in all my previous experiences of the Trance Condition, and there is no accounting for it.

Over a year elapsed before I could repeat this success and then in October, 1909, I have another record :

After the sun had set, I lay down on the sofa to experiment. My eyes were closed ; but presently, with my astral sight, I could see the room quite plainly and my wife sitting sewing by the fire. I also felt a numbness creeping up my legs and the old disinclination, or inability, to move. This told me I had attained the Trance Condition. As before, I just willed to leave my body and then found myself standing on the lamplit pavement outside the house. I walked along the street for a short distance and entered a grocer's shop. This was full of customers, but no one took any notice of me. I wished to see whether I should be visible to the grocer ; but my body called me back, and I thought that I woke. The room seemed just as real as in waking life, but at that moment a brightly plumaged parrot flew over my head and through the wall. I then knew, from observing this illusion, that I had experienced the False Awakening and was still in the Trance Condition. However, before I could make another excursion some noise broke the trance.

To this period belongs my only experiment with chloroform. Having obtained about a teaspoonful from a medical friend, I poured a little on a cotton-wool pad and proceeded very cautiously to inhale it. I was lying on the sofa, and my wife and Barrow were present. After a few sniffs, it seemed to me that I shot up to the stars, and that a shining silver thread connected my celestial self with my physical body. Dual consciousness was very pronounced. When I spoke, it seemed to me that my words travelled down the thread and were then spoken by my physical self ; but the process was simultaneous, and I could feel myself among the stars and on the sofa at one and the same time. From this Olympian height I discoursed to my small audience ; but alas, the great brain was clouded ! I am told that I manifested a regrettable flippancy, and that my remarks did not constitute a valuable contribution worthy of preservation in the annals of Psychical Research. Also, after the experiment, I was for a few minutes extremely unwell. Therefore, all things considered, I cannot recommend the chloroform method of obtaining separation to the serious student.

In 1909, too, I find a record of a rather quaint little Dream of Knowledge :

I dreamed that my wife and I awoke, got up, and dressed. On pulling up the blind, we made the amazing discovery that the row of houses opposite had vanished and in their place were bare fields. I said to my wife, "This means I am dreaming, though everything seems so real and I feel perfectly awake. Those houses could not disappear in the night, and look at all that grass !" But though my wife was greatly puzzled, I could not convince her it was a dream. "Well," I continued, "I am prepared to stand by my reason and put it to the test. I will jump out of the window, and I shall take no harm." Ruthlessly ignoring her pleading and objecting, I opened the window and climbed out on to the sill. I then jumped, and floated gently down into the street. When my feet touched the pavement, I awoke. My wife had no memory of dreaming.

As a matter of fact, I was very nervous about jumping ; for the atmosphere *inside* our bedroom seemed so absolutely real that it nearly made me accept the manifest absurdity of things outside. Was my dream-wife only the creation of my mind ?—or was she actually my wife functioning in her astral

vehicle ?   I do not know.   As will be seen later, it is a
problem I have never been able to solve.   Most unfortunately, my wife has never had any memory of
dreaming on the occasions when I have seemed to
encounter her either in a projection experience or in an
ordinary dream.   There is a contrariness about things ;
for once, being probably in the trance state herself, she
was frightened by seeing my etheric or astral self sitting
up out of my recumbent physical form, and then of
course I could not remember anything.

I have also a note of a telepathic experience.   One
night, after supper, I went out for a stroll and was
much absorbed by the theme of a story I was then
writing.   I was smoking the very strong tobacco I
affected in those days, and I puffed away mechanically
as I pondered over my plot.   Just as I was passing an
advertisement hoarding in the Westminster Bridge
Road I caught myself swaying and thought I should be
sick.   In a few minutes I mastered the situation, put
away the offending pipe, and resumed my walk.   When
I got home I had almost forgotten the incident and was
surprised to find my wife quite anxious about me.   It
seemed she had had a sudden mental vision, in which
she saw me reeling as I passed this particular hoarding,
and got a very vivid impression that I had been taken
ill.   I could not remember having thought of her at
all, being so preoccupied with my story up to the point
where I discovered I had oversmoked ; nor could she
remember thinking of me until the mental picture suddenly intruded on her consciousness.   The trivial
nature of the incident adds to the difficulty of finding
a satisfactory explanation.   Once, when I was in really

grave danger, my wife sensed my perilous position and was in great distress ; yet there was no mental picture, and she had not the slightest idea as to the nature of my predicament, despite the fact that she was very much in my thoughts at the time.

In the August of 1911 we returned to Southampton, where we had many friends and sentimental associations, and my next record is in July, 1912 :

I was lying on the bed in the afternoon when I experienced the False Awakening, imagining that my wife and two friends were sitting in the room and talking. I felt too tired to take any part in this conversation and "went to sleep" again. When I next became aware of my surroundings I realized that I was in the Trance Condition and could leave my body. I therefore sat up (out of my body, as it were) and then leisurely got off the bed. Dual consciousness was very strong. I could feel myself lying on the bed and standing by it, my legs pressing against the coverlet, simultaneously ; but though I could see all the objects in the room quite clearly, I could not see my body when I looked for it upon the bed. Everything seemed just as real as in waking life—more so, extra vivid—and I felt indescribably well and free, my brain seeming extraordinarily alert. I left the bed and walked slowly round the room to the door, the sense of dual consciousness diminishing as I moved farther away from my body ; but just as I was going to leave the room, my body pulled me back instantaneously and the trance was broken. There was no final stage of apparent catalepsy, and I experienced no unpleasant after-effects.

This record does not seem very interesting ; but it

marked an important advance, and its special significance lies in the *gentle* way in which separation was
effected. It was my first experience of a non-instantaneous projection, made when in a state of self-induced trance and without the preliminary Dream of
Knowledge. It is my plan to deal with my advances in
chronological order ; but though the reference will be
obscure at this stage, I should like to add that this was
really a "Pineal Door" projection, and the painful
business of getting through the "door" was accomplished while I was unconscious on the physical plane.
It will be seen that these remarks also apply to other
examples of non-instantaneous projection.

An Instantaneous Projection is the name I have given
to the kind where separation is effected by more or
less forcibly ejecting the subtle vehicle from the
physical body by a strong effort of will. In these
cases the apparent speed is so great that one passes
through the walls of the room in a flash, and thus there
is no time for the sensation of dual consciousness.
Often, too, in this method, breaks in consciousness will
occur, so that the experimenter may not be fully aware
of his conditions, identity, etc., until he comes to rest
perhaps seemingly many miles away from his body.

It will be noted that I could not see my body when I
looked for it upon the bed, and this has been my general
experience, yet other projectionists state they can see
theirs. It has been suggested to me that if I am functioning in my astral body, I should be able to see only
the astral counterparts of the objects in the room ;
and therefore to see my physical body a sort of "downward clairvoyance" would be necessary, as its astral

counterpart would be no longer coincident with it. Perhaps other people have this power and I do not possess it. But, fundamentally, different states of consciousness are the result of being able to respond to different rates of vibration; and for this reason it may be the projectionist when exteriorized lives to some extent in a world of his own, and no two experimenters will ever get precisely similar results, because they will not both respond to exactly the same range of vibrations. This is true, but to a much smaller degree, even in waking life. Our physical world is by no means the same place for all of us, even though there is sufficient general agreement about the phenomena it presents to enable us to get on with the business side of things. Some people are colour-blind, others tone-deaf; and if several people witness the same happening and their separate impressions are recorded, remarkable differences occur in their narratives. Small wonder then that when we get away from good old solid matter, we find the impressions or experiences of one projectionist are not in complete agreement with those of another.

Mr. Sylvan Muldoon, in his book *The Case for Astral Projection*, The Aries Press, Chicago, 1936, writes as follows :

"Mr. Fox maintained that while projected he never could see his physical body—although he could see his wife's very plainly. This fact has been pointed out to me often in the past as evidence against the reality of his exteriorizations. While, as I have pointed out, I am not resorting to explanations in this present volume, there is nothing unusual about this fact whatever. There are many reasons why this could be true which in fact strengthen, rather than weaken, Mr. Fox's account. In a subsequent volume this will be fully explained."

There was, however, just one occasion on which I was able to see my body. The projection, which was of the instantaneous kind, was made in a very unusual way :

February 15, 1914.   *Foundry Lane, Southampton*

In the afternoon I was experimenting seated in a deck-chair. Presently I got into the right Trance Condition, seeing with the astral sight though my eyes were tightly closed. I willed to ascend. Then suddenly I seemed to be wafted out of my body, turned so that I faced it, and borne upwards in a position almost horizontal. In this rapid passage upwards I saw my face as though viewed from only an inch away, strange and monstrous, yet unmistakably mine. And through the closed eyelids the eyeballs were plainly visible. They were rolled upwards, thus showing only the whites, which added to the gruesome effect. This apparition was so unexpected and ghastly that I was startled. Nevertheless I continued to will to ascend, and shot up into blackness. Then, when I was thinking of taking the next step, the trance ended. The shock had proved too much for my mental control of the situation. The peculiar closeness of the view-point may have rendered my face visible to me on this one occasion.

CHAPTER VII

EIGHT RECORDS

THE years 1913, 1914 and 1915 saw my interest in my projection experiments steadily increasing. I had written two novels, which were destined never to be published, and then tried my luck with short stories. By 1913 these were going fairly well ; that is to say, seven out of every nine written found a home after anything up to eighteen rejections ! But once I had got over the novelty of seeing my name in print, my natural perverseness asserted itself and my interest waned. The stories I enjoyed writing were always the most difficult to sell, and the stories which sold comparatively easily I grew weary of writing. But with the coming of the Great War my literary problem was solved : nothing would sell but war stuff, and my artistic soul shrank from the "mugging up" I should have to do to write this. So I got a clerical job and devoted my spare hours to occult studies and research work, the Army having refused my services for the time being.

The dearth of records is now over and I have plenty of material to select from, both of successful projections and of trance experiences which were terminated before separation was achieved. In the present chapter I have chosen eight records from this period, each of which seems to me to possess features of especial interest.

The reader is warned not to take my statements on the pineal gland too literally ; indeed, if it please him, he is welcome to look upon the Pineal Door as purely imaginary ; but, at least, this conception forms a very useful aid to a mental exercise which undoubtedly leads to a new form of consciousness—even if the projection theory is rejected. The result I obtained is beyond all question ; but my explanation of the actual process involved may be more symbolical than accurate. However, I have reason to suppose that I am not far out in my description, always remembering that things are only relatively true, and that the *truth* must ever elude the spoken or written word. And it is quite immaterial to the success of the experiment. By employing this method the result *can* be obtained.

Autumn, 1913.   *Foundry Lane, Southampton*

In the afternoon, intending to experiment, I lay down on the bed and succeeded in getting into the Trance Condition. I then proceeded to leave my body, dual consciousness being experienced until I had passed out of the house (by going through the closed doors) ; but on reaching the street I could not feel my physical body lying upon the bed. I had walked on for about a hundred yards, apparently unobserved by the few people about, when I was caught up in some strong current and borne away with great velocity. I came to rest on a beautiful but unknown common. There seemed to be a school-treat going on ; for there were many children, dressed in white, playing games and having tea beneath the trees. There were also some adults present—in particular I noticed one old gipsy woman. Bluish smoke rose up from the fires they had lit, and a magnificent amber sunset cast a mellow golden glow upon the peaceful scene. I walked on until I came to some red brick houses, which evidently marked the limit of the common in that direction. The front door of one of these houses was half-open, so I entered, curious to see if the inhabitants would become aware of my intrusion. At the end of the hall was a flight of richly carpeted stairs. Up these I passed.

Seeing a door ajar on the first landing, I entered and found myself in a comfortably furnished bedroom. A young lady, dressed in claret-coloured velvet, was standing with her back to me, tidying her hair before a mirror. I could see that radiant amber sky through the window by the dressing-table, and the girl's rich auburn tresses were gleaming redly in this glamorous light. I noticed that the coverlet of the bed had a crumpled appearance and that there was water in a basin on the washstand. "Ah, my lady," thought I, "you too have been lying down, and now you are making yourself presentable for tea—or is it dinner?"

I did not mind intruding upon her privacy ; for she might have no existence outside of my brain, and I knew, from previous experiences, that there was small likelihood of my being visible to her. It occurred to me that I would stand just behind her and look over her shoulder into the mirror. I wanted to see whether it would reflect my face. I stood so close to her that I was conscious of a pleasant fragrance emanating from her hair, or perhaps from the soap she had recently used. In the mirror I could see her face—a good-looking one, I think her eyes were grey—but not the faintest indication of mine was visible.

"Well," I thought, "you evidently cannot see me. Can you feel me ?"

And I laid a hand upon her shoulder. I distinctly felt the softness of her velvet dress, and then she gave a violent start—so violent that I in my turn was startled too. Instantly my body drew me back and I was awake, my condition being immediately normal—no duration of trance, or cataleptic sensations. No bad after-effects. The western sky was blue when I lay down ; but on breaking the trance I saw that it was actually the same glorious amber colour it had been in my out-of-the-body experience. Unfortunately, I omitted the date of this experiment, though I wrote the account immediately afterwards.

From the point of view that to prolong the experience should be the first consideration, touching the lady was certainly a mistake. I have often found that, though I may be invisible to the people I encounter in my dream-travelling, they respond readily to touch. If the shock produced is great enough to affect me, then my body calls me back—probably through repercussion.

Note : Projection is at present in its infancy ; but if in the future it should become a fairly common accomplishment, this question of one's right to intrude, even in an unseen body, upon the privacy of another person will have to receive serious consideration. I think such an intrusion as mine, deliberately made, is really indefensible conduct for any person who has become convinced that projection is a truth. However, owing to the strong astral currents and the fact that most often one has little or no control over the out-of-the-body experience, it seems to me that accidental intrusions are unavoidable. This much is clear : unless we are quite sure that a friend would not be frightened, or object to receiving an astral visit, we should not attempt to reach another person without his consent. Once permission had been obtained, it would be better for evidential reasons not to acquaint the percipient with the time of the proposed visit, but to place a written statement, enclosed in a sealed envelope, in the hands of a third party before making the experiment.

December 14, 1913.   *Foundry Lane, Southampton*

I was walking through some side-streets in a place that might have been a hitherto unexplored portion of the vast dream-London, and I knew that I was dreaming. No one was abroad but me, though it was bright daylight, the cloudless sky being a delightful pale azure. So I emerged into a mighty square, and there before me towered a colossal building—a miracle of bulk and architectural beauty. Roughly it was Gothic in design, a mass of lacework and carven detail, with innumerable pointed windows and countless niches holding statues. The whole glowed with an indescribable mellowness, compounded of a thousand subtle shades and tints, in the wonderful brilliance and purity of the dream-light. This building was not only a thing of brick and stone ; it seemed to be a living thing, to have an eternal soul ; and for me it had all the high, intensely spiritual appeal of a lovely woman. That building alone might have inspired a novel, which one could call "The Pinnacled Glory"—borrowing from Browning's *Abt Vogler*. Near it was a grey, decaying statue (perhaps of Queen Victoria) upon a massive pedestal ; but this structure, though about fifty or sixty feet high, seemed absurdly small—a mere dwarf —beside the amazing loftiness of this enormous building.

The statue had the appearance of being very old—a thing belonging to past centuries.   As I greatly wished to reach the summit of this beautiful building, I decided to levitate and made the slight paddling motions, which I have hitherto found necessary, at the same time leaning backwards as though about to float on water.   At first I rose slowly, then I seemed to be caught in some strong current and was borne up with great velocity in a slanting direction.   I remember passing close to the face of the statue—a monstrous, weather-beaten, ghastly thing, which had the appearance of having been eaten away by some loathsome disease, the crumbling nostrils making the nose grotesquely pointed—and the little images in the niches grew suddenly large as I swept up and up.   Then, when it seemed that I in my diagonal course must penetrate the building, my body called me back and I awoke. The glamour of this experience persisted for the best part of the day.

Note : Unlike the Bletchingden Bay adventure, in which I seemed to be earthbound, the above experience was located on some level of the astral plane.   In the course of my various explorations of this place I have found that the astral counterpart (if such it be) of a city appears much larger than the earthly one ; for in addition to its present structures and features are to be found buildings, monuments, etc., which have no present existence on the earth. Some of these may have existed in the past ; and others I suspect to be very powerful thought-forms—or perhaps the astral foreshadowings of earthly buildings yet to come. To the uninitiated this will sound very nonsensical ; but consider it this way—every enterprise has its horoscope, the key to the occult forces behind its inception. If you can become connected up with the psychic trail of the forces governing the Xtown Technical College, you may get a vision of the new buildings to be occupied by that institution in 1960—which is what a psychometrist actually does. Was it not written long ago that Past, Present, and Future are in truth but *one* ? Well, the astral plane is an infinite network of psychic trails, and Xtown, as a whole, also has its horoscope. I do not wish to labour the point. To the astral explorer, then, Xtown will seem at once both familiar and strange, a curious blend of known and unknown, of old-style and new or ultra-new ; and the general effect will be that the astral Xtown is much larger than the earthly one. And as far as my experiences go, the investigator, who makes his *n*th trip to the astral Xtown, will still find the same features (non-existent on earth) that puzzled him on his first adventure.

July 9, 1914.   *Foundry Lane, Southampton*

At 9 a.m. I lay down on my bed to experiment in dream-travelling. Events happened as follows :

(1) I fell asleep and dreamed that I awoke ; this False Awakening being followed by my actually waking.

(2) I dozed off again, and this time I succeeded in getting into the right state of trance, and I was perfectly conscious of my condition. I then left my body (but could not see it on the bed) and crossed the room to the door. Dual consciousness very strong : I could feel myself lying on the bed and standing by the door at one and the same time. I passed into the hall, then opened the front door and closed it ; but of course it was not the real physical door that I opened. At this point the dual consciousness ceased and I could no longer feel my body upon the bed. Intending to pay an astral visit to some friends close by, I walked for about a hundred yards up Foundry Lane towards Shirley Avenue. I passed a girl who did not see me. However, before I could reach the Avenue, I was caught up by some force and borne away with immense velocity, finally coming to rest in a strange town.

Unseen, I passed along a busy street, observing with interest the unfamiliar buildings and the heedless people. In particular, I remember one front garden, where a miniature wind-vane worked a curious little dancing Punchinello. I crossed a very grimy railway bridge. Green locomotives were shining in the brilliant sunlight ; and I noticed how beautiful were the clouds of condensing steam from the funnels, pearly clouds against the azure sky. So I walked for about a quarter of a mile, then I began to feel my feet grow heavy. Heavier and heavier they became. My body was tugging hard—that body lying on the bed perhaps many miles away. At last I could withstand the call no longer. It was as though a mighty cord of stretched elastic, connecting my two bodies, had suddenly come into existence and overpowered me. I shot backwards at an amazing speed, entering my body so violently that the trance was instantly broken. I awoke.

(3) I fell asleep again and had several quite ordinary and uninteresting dreams, in which I had no knowledge of dreaming. I woke once more.

(4) I got into the proper Trance Condition again, fully conscious that I was in it. Left my body—phenomena as before, under (2)—and passed out into the garden. I then decided that I would make my first attempt at "skrying" or "rising through the planes". I stood erect, arms to my sides, and concentrating all my will-power in one supreme effort, I willed to ascend. The effect was truly surprising. Instantly the earth fell from my feet—that was how it seemed to me, because of the suddenness and speed of my ascent. I looked down on my home, now no bigger than a matchbox ; the streets were now only thick lines separating the houses. I noted that I was travelling in a slanting direction. I rectified this by an effort of the will and continued to ascend straight up. Soon the earth was hidden by white clouds. Up and up and up. Velocity ever increasing. The loneliness I felt was indescribable. Up and up and up. My consciousness was perfect, except for one thing—I lost my sense of *time*. I might have been out of my body for hours, or even a day—I could not tell. Thoughts of premature burial haunted me. Up and up and up. This loneliness was dreadful ; only those who have had a similar experience can realize what I felt.

The blue of the sky had been gradually fading ; but the brilliance of the light had not diminished—at least, to any marked degree.   Now I saw a most awe-inspiring phenomenon : from a point on the zenith emerged a succession of shimmering, leaden-hued concentric circles of light, ever spreading in huge ripples—as when a stone is thrown into a pond.   At this sight I got really frightened, but I did not lose my self-control. Realizing that I had nearly reached the limit to my powers of endurance, I willed to descend.   Instantly the process was reversed ; the sky grew blue again ; earth came into sight through the fleecy veil of clouds and rose up to meet my feet.   I passed again into the house and gently entered my body.   I then experienced a touch of catalepsy and had the illusion that my wife was embracing me, trying desperately to bring me back to life.   Actually she was not in the house.

I broke the trance without much difficulty and rose from the bed.   It was noon ; so the whole experiment had lasted three hours.   I felt no sickness or bad after-effects.   Indeed, I had an unusual sense of physical freshness and spiritual exaltation which lasted for the rest of the day.   Actually the sun was shining brilliantly throughout my experiment, and so it was in my experiences outside of my body.

Note : The travelling upwards, or skrying, must not be confused with the clumsy attempts at levitation made by me in some dreams in which I have had the knowledge of dreaming.   In these latter, levitation was effected by beating down or paddling motions of the hands and arms, the body leaning backwards at an angle as though about to float on water.   In these cases the apparent height reached was only about fifty to one hundred feet, and then the pull of my physical body, or some force similar to gravitation, would make me descend.

When I had reached my maximum height I could turn over, so that I faced the ground beneath me, and then proceed by making swimming motions or by will-power alone if the conditions were favourable. Indeed, I think that the real motive power is in the will alone and that the motions of the hands, arms and legs, are only aids to concentration and may therefore be dispensed with if one's condition is fully realized. Skrying, however, is accomplished by a supreme effort of the will alone, and the results obtained are very different.

While attempts at dream-levitation are quite harmless, true skrying—such as that accomplished by me in the above experiment—is, I believe, a very dangerous proceeding and not to be lightly or frivolously undertaken.

Skrying is like gliding, but in a vertical direction. There is no downward pull analagous to gravity, but only the call of the body. It is done by a purely mental effort, the arms being quite passive, and it is characterized by an enormous velocity of ascent. I have been told that by using this method it is possible to travel to other planets ; but that it is extremely dangerous for a student who is not under the guidance of an Adept. In skrying I have advanced no further than I did in this first experience. I tell myself that a married man must exercise some prudence in pursuing these investigations, but, really, I am afraid.

Other projectionists state that they can see this

elastic cord, which connects the exteriorized vehicle with the physical body, and even describe it in some detail. I have struggled against the pull of it often enough, but I have never been able to see it—if we exclude the chloroform episode. It is interesting to note that when the trance is terminated involuntarily, and therefore suddenly, the effect is that one is drawn *backwards* to the physical body, but the speed is so great that the return seems almost instantaneous.

June 13, 1915.   *New Road, Southampton*

In the afternoon I lay down on a couch, with a view to experimenting. Got into the trance state. My eyes were closed, but I could see the room very clearly. On attempting to leave my body, I experienced very peculiar and rather terrifying preliminary sensations— like a great outrush or uprush of all my being. Separation was excellently effected. Dual consciousness until I left the room. I walked downstairs. Then I was caught up and borne away to what seemed to be a large oriental palace. A beautiful girl was dancing before an assembly of reclining, richly garbed men and women. No one could see me. I stood before the dancer and looked into her sky-blue eyes, but she took no notice. Foolishly succumbing to her fascination, I placed my arm around her bare, warm waist. She started so violently that the shock induced in me broke the trance. Instantly I rushed back to my body and awoke. Thus, through gratifying the senses, my experiment came to an untimely end.

Note : This record is of especial interest, for it marks my first conscious experience of a Pineal Door projection. Later I shall list all the phenomena I have noted in connection with this form of projection. The reader may be inclined to ask the question : How is it that certain features became evident only in successive experiments ? Why could not the whole process be grasped at this first experience ? I think the answer to that question lies in the following considerations :

(1) Until one has become accustomed to it, the actual process of passing through the "Door" in the pineal gland produces an effect of extreme mental confusion and a terrible fear. Indeed, one feels that one is heading straight for death or insanity.

(2) In addition to this the sounds peculiar to the Trance Condition (see Chapter V) distract one's attention and increase the general confusion.

(3) Breaks in consciousness occur, so that such things as the cerebral "clicks" (see Chapter III) will often be missed.

(4) After the return to the body, one is dependent upon the physical brain for the memories retained of the whole experience, and the impressions often become blurred, or wiped out by others, or fail altogether to register on the brain substance—especially if the return be abrupt.

June 28, 1915.   *Foundry Lane, Southampton*

Before dawn I experimented in astral projection. I obtained separation—i.e. left my body—six times. During the whole experiment my trance remained unbroken. Each time I returned to my body I strengthened the trance by will-power, so that it got deeper and deeper, my body becoming seemingly as rigid as a corpse. Finally I broke the trance myself, because I was not sure how much time had been occupied in my journeys, and I feared it might prove dangerous to delay my return any longer. My experiences out of my body were vivid and varied. I could have written a fairly long account of them, had I made notes immediately on breaking the trance ; but when I dressed, several hours later, and after two or three ordinary dreams, most of the details of my travels had slipped away. Very roughly, what happened was as follows :

(1) Left my body and stood by the bed, watching what might have been my wife's astral vehicle or some spirit or elemental impersonating her. She was walking about the room, and I could not see her body on the bed, but she did not take any notice of me. Returned to my body.

(2) Left my body and passed out of the room. Ascended the stairs and encountered the astral vehicle of Mrs. S., who lived in the same house. She did not see me. At this point I experienced a sudden transition to a strange room, where I met two young ladies whom I have never seen in waking life. Returned to my body.

(3) Left my body and returned to the same strange house. There I had a short conversation with the two young ladies, who were still in the same room. Returned to my body.

(4) Left my body and passed out of the house. Sudden transition to a strange town or city. Night, and the streets crowded. Moved about unseen by the people. I rode for some distance on a tram, but the

conductor did not see me. Read a recruiting poster in English. Returned to my body.

(5) Left my body and passed out of the house. Sudden transition to an oriental city. Bright day. Crowds of natives, who looked like Indians, and some Europeans. Street bazaars and shining white oriental buildings. In the distance I could see a curious fountain : a huge, kneeling elephant, sculptured in black stone, ejected from its curled-back trunk a shower of water, which was caught in a white shell-shaped basin. Returned to my body.

(6) Left my body and sat by the window, gazing out at a bright setting moon and meditating where I would go next. So far, owing to the gradual deepening of the trance, my out-of-the-body periods had been each time of longer duration. Decided that I had better terminate the experiment. Returned to my body and broke the trance by a steady effort of the will.

Awake at last, I got out of bed and looked at the moon. It was just as I had seen it when out of my body a few minutes earlier. The initial trance experiences and the final return to waking life were slightly unpleasant ; but, when separation had been attained, the results were highly pleasurable by reason of the delightful feeling of perfect freedom, health and clarity of perception. On the whole, then, this prolonged series of experiments was remarkably successful.

Note : This record is given as it was written in 1915. After this length of time I cannot remember how the first separation was effected, but it was most certainly a gentle one. Probably I was unconscious during the passing of the Pineal Door and found myself in that state where separation was only a matter of sitting up out of my physical body and then getting off the bed.

Owing to obvious time discrepancies—for I was experimenting in the early hours of the morning, between 2 and 3 a.m.—episode (4) must have been astral in nature, as it seemed to be in England ; but the others may have had an earthly location. People who cannot forget or forgive poor Raymond's cigar will get very cross with me when I say that there are electric trams on the astral plane ; but there *are*—unless there is no astral plane, and my trams run only in my brain.

December 15, 1915.   *Foundry Lane, Southampton*

Last night in a dream in which my wife figured, I got to know that I was dreaming through the unexpected appearance of a large model battleship which was propelled through the streets by men walking inside it. We witnessed interesting and strange carnival scenes and a big fire, a great building being ablaze. Eventually we left the carnival and fire behind us and came to a yellow path, leading across a desolate moor. As we stood at the foot of this path it suddenly rose up before us and became a roadway of golden light stretching from earth to zenith.

Now in this amber-tinted shining haze there appeared countless coloured forms of men and beasts, representing man's upward evolution through different stages of civilization. These forms faded away ; the pathway lost its golden tint and became a mass of vibrating circles or globules (like frog's eggs), a purplish-blue in colour. These in their turn changed to "peacock's eyes"; and then suddenly there came a culminating vision of a gigantic peacock, whose outspread tail filled the heavens. I exclaimed to my wife, "The Vision of the Universal Peacock !" Moved by the splendour of the sight, I recited in a loud voice a mantra. Then the dream ended.

On passing from this Dream of Knowledge, I experienced the False Awakening. Later I found myself in the Trance Condition and proceeded to experiment. I obtained separation and left my body. I then saw my wife's astral vehicle (which was much altered), or an impersonation of her, seated in a chair. We talked for a while about astrology and the Isis worship of Ancient Egypt. Presently I was torn by what seemed to be cross currents of occult forces. I heard great noises and experienced a horrible fear. Thus I was drawn back to my physical body which was in the cataleptic state, but at first I could not break the trance. I suffered considerable pain through the rending effect of these great forces. I also had the illusion that my wife (in her physical body) was anxious about me and that I was actually speaking to her, explaining my condition. When I broke the trance I found her still asleep ; but I cannot tell if I had really spoken. There were no bad after-effects. Unfortunately, my wife had no memory of the dream or of our astral meeting and conversation.

February 6, 1916.   *Foundry Lane, Southampton*

On this occasion I experimented with a definite object, to visit Mrs. X at her house in Lumsden Avenue, Southampton. On retiring for the night, I lay on my right side, keeping as still as possible and taking deep rhythmic breaths. I did not concentrate on Mrs. X., but on the preliminary stages of the experiment, as I wanted to pass into the Trance Condition without losing consciousness even for a moment. In this I was quite successful. After the breathing had continued for some time, I noted a curious sensation in my physical eyes, as though they were rolled upwards and squinting slightly. At the same time all my consciousness seemed to be focussed upon some point situated in the middle of my brain, perhaps in the region of the pineal gland. It occurred to me that I was "concentrating inwardly," as some occult students term it. For some time I continued this concentration, and more and more it seemed to me that all my incorporeal self was being condensed about this central point within my physical brain. Soon I began to feel a numbness stealing over my body, extending from the feet upwards and gradually stiffening into a painful rigidity. I now seemed to be in a state resembling catalepsy, even my jaws being bound together, as though the muscles had changed into iron clamps. I was still in darkness, my physical eyes being tightly closed and rolled upwards ; but now I had the sensation of possessing another pair, and these non-physical or astral eyes I opened. It will thus be seen that I actually passed from waking life into the proper trance condition without any break in my consciousness.

My physical body was lying entranced on its right side and facing my wife. As I opened my astral eyes, I turned right round within my physical body so that I faced the other direction. Great forces seemed to be straining the atmosphere, and bluish-green flashes of light came from all parts of the room. I then caught sight of a hideous monster—a vague, white, filmy, formless thing, spreading out in queer patches and snake-like protuberances. It had two enormous round eyes, like globes filled with pale blue fire, each about six or seven inches in diameter. I was certainly very frightened. I felt my physical heart leap, and my breathing changed suddenly to jerky gaspings. However, my reason conquered my fear. I turned over again within my physical body, so that the monster was out of sight. Telling myself that nothing could harm me, I concentrated my will on prolonging the trance, which the shock had very nearly broken. In this I was successful. My heart became normal again, and my breathing rhythmic.

Once more I turned within myself and viewed the room. The monster had gone, but the flashings continued for a little while. These too subsided, and then the room seemed just as usual, except for the fact that it was dimly and evenly illuminated by no visible source of light. I then sat up in my astral body, thus raising myself out of the recumbent physical, swung my legs over the side of the bed and finally stood up, having effected complete separation. Dual consciousness was most pronounced, I could distinctly feel myself lying on the bed and standing on the floor at the same time. However, I could not see my body on the bed, perhaps because its astral counterpart had been withdrawn with me—but this is only theory. My wife's form was plainly visible. I bent over and kissed her, and she opened her eyes, regarding me sleepily. It then occurred to me that I had better get on with my experiment, so I waved my hand to her and left the room.

Passing through both room door and front door, I stood outside the house and paused while I concentrated all my will-power upon the idea of travelling to Mrs. X. At this point I had a brief glimpse of a barely visible curtain of vibrating circular objects—resembling frog's eggs. I think they were a misty blue or purple in colour, but they were just on the border of visibility. I had now lost the sensation of dual consciousness. All of me seemed to be outside the house. My reason told me that my physical body was lying on the bed beside my wife, but I no longer felt it there. Small time was necessary for this concentration on the idea of travelling to Mrs. X.

Almost immediately I was caught up and borne along with ever-increasing velocity, passing through houses and trees, and apparently taking the shortest path to the desired goal. At the end of this journey, which occupied only a second or so, if that, I found myself beating against the fronts of houses resembling those in Lumsden Avenue. I was like a piece of paper blown by a gale hither and thither. The directing impulse seemed to have suddenly given out, and I could not find the right house. At this point my body called me back. I made the journey home in a flash and found myself still in the Trance Condition and experiencing dual consciousness.

I concentrated for a while on strengthening the trance, as I intended to try again. Just as I was about to leave my body, I heard my wife say with peculiar distinctness: "No ! You must not do it again now, or I shall be frightened." I thought her voice was probably only an illusion and so hesitated. Then she spoke again : "Wake up, dear !" I still thought the voice was most likely unreal in the physical sense ; but not wishing to run any risk of distressing her, I obeyed. I broke the trance quite easily and questioned her. She had not spoken and had no recollection of seeing me leave my body.

Note : This was the first time I had succeeded in passing from the waking state into the Trance Condition without experiencing a break in consciousness. I was thus able to observe the successive stages involved, which makes this experiment of particular value. Nevertheless, once the trance state had been reached, despite the apparent continuity of the experience, I think there must have been some break in my consciousness if only for a minute fraction of time. For the leisurely and easy manner in which separation was effected points to this having been a true Pineal Door projection, yet I had no memory of actually passing through this hypothetical door or of hearing the "click" as it shut behind me. It should be mentioned that at this date I was unaware of the precise position of Mrs. X's house, though I knew the locality roughly, and I had not seen her.

On visiting Mrs. X for the first time, I recognized the houses above and below hers as similar to those against which I had found myself beating in my experiment, but hers was of a different design. Finally, it should be noted that my wife, functioning in her astral vehicle, might have seen me leave my body and also have spoken to me and yet have retained no memory (registered on her physical brain) when suddenly awakened by my voice questioning her. I have frequently found that a sudden return to waking life prevents one from bringing through any details of the dream that has been so rudely ended. The "monster" may have been some form of elemental or non-human entity.

Another incident connected with Mrs. X is worthy of record : On the night of March 15, 1916, I dreamed much of Mrs. X. In the morning, although I could recall no details, I felt I had made astral contact with her. There was, however, one thing I could remember, that some time in the night I had been accompanied by a small, black, furry animal, which might have been a dog. On this same night Mrs. X. lying awake in bed, was disturbed by a scratching and pattering sound in her room. On rising and switching on the light, she, being clairvoyant, distinctly saw a small, black, furry animal, which ran to the fireplace, rattled the fire-irons, and then vanished in the grate. After this, despite the bright light, the noises continued and a picture was persistently rattled against the wall.

Mrs. X turned off the light and went to bed again, and then the noises ceased. Now, although she had no material reason whatever to connect me with these manifestations, she said that she could feel my presence in the room and believed the phenomena were caused by a force emanating from me. She gave me the above account, my wife being present, *before* I had mentioned my dream and the animal.

April 10, 1916.   *Foundry Lane, Southampton*

Before dawn I experienced the False Awakening. Illusions of sound and a great sensation of fear made me aware that I was really in the Trance Condition. Knowing this, my fear passed and I decided to experiment. I concentrated on the attempt to leave my body, and the result was most interesting. I felt my incorporeal self rushing towards, and being condensed in, the pineal gland—at least, this was the sensation—and at the same time the golden astral light blazed up and became very brilliant ; then my body pulled me back, and the astral light died down again, the sensation being precisely the reverse of the previous one—i.e. my incorporeal self rushed back, away from the pineal gland and expanding, until it coincided with the physical body once more. I concentrated again and the same thing happened, but at the third attempt I succeeded in obtaining separation. Once this had been effected, the astral light became normal again.

I then moved off the bed and tried to feel with my astral hand my physical body lying in the trance, but I could neither feel nor see it. At this point a voice, apparently emanating from my wife, whom I could see, pleaded with me not to experiment any further. Knowing from previous experience that this voice—with regard to my wife's physical body—was very probably only an illusion, I chose to disregard it. I then walked across the room and was surprised to find myself stopped by the wall, which seemed as solid as in ordinary waking life. Now usually, in my out-of-the-body adventures, I can pass through walls without being conscious of any appreciable effort ; but this time, for some unknown reason, the conditions seemed altered. I stood facing the wall, gently pressing against it, and steadily willed to pass through it. I succeeded, and the sensation was most curious. Pre-serving full consciousness, I seemed to pass like a gas—in a spread-out condition—through the interstices between the molecules of the wall, regaining my normal proportions on the other side.

I then willed to travel to a certain temple which I have been told once existed in Allahabad. I moved off at a great speed and came to rest in a modern brilliantly lighted room. Here a man and a woman were seated at a table, having a meal. They did not seem to see me. Again I repeated my desire : "Temple—Allahabad—India—in the Past". And now it seemed to me there was a sort of hole or break formed in the continuity of the astral matter ; and through this, in the distance—as though viewed through a very long tunnel—I could see something indistinct which might have been an entrance to a temple, with a statue still further away showing through it. I then moved forward again, but to my disappointment came to rest almost immediately in another room, where three women were seated at a table which also bore the remains of a meal. A fourth woman—pretty, with fair hair and blue eyes—was standing up in the act of leaving the table. Apparently, none of them could see me.

Sticking to my objective, I once more repeated : "Temple—Allahabad—India—in the Past". The tunnel arrangement was coming into view again, then something must have occurred which broke my trance—though what, I do not know. Instantly I rushed back to my body and awoke.

Note : The wall incident is decidedly curious. My

wife has suggested an ingenious explanation, based on Mrs. X's belief that I have mediumistic powers. My wife thinks, then, that I may have actually materialized to some extent my out-of-the-body self on this occasion, drawing the matter from my entranced physical body, which she thinks might account for my unexpected difficulty in passing through the wall. The physical particles would have to be dematerialized, or more finely divided, to pass through the physical wall. An ingenious idea, though perhaps far-fetched. The truth is, I have so much to learn about the conditions obtaining in this astral or dream-world.

There are certainly unknown forces working, and these may at times greatly affect the results of my experiments. On some occasions everything goes very smoothly ; on others, unexpected obstacles or retarding elements become manifest. One point in conclusion : If this world in which I find myself in my projection experiments exists only in my imagination, as the scientific sceptic would insist, why did I not reach this Indian temple with which I was mentally familiar ? Instead, I found myself in these strange and totally unexpected rooms. Why ?

CHAPTER VIII

THAT attempt to reach the temple in Allahabad was destined to be my last conscious Pineal Door projection—at least, up to the time of writing this book. As will be seen later, I am still able to obtain separation by the Instantaneous Method. The next time I tried to induce the Trance Condition, I found that always before my inner eyes was the vision of a black *crux ansata* ; and now my magic would not work, the "trap-door" *would not open*. The *crux ansata* could not be dispelled. When I closed my eyes and turned to the light, the symbol showed clear-cut, as though painted in black on the red field of my eyelids. With my eyes open, in a dim light, I could still see it as though it were projected in front of me. And try as I might I could no longer pass the Pineal Door.

Soon after this I started a long investigation into the powers of a most remarkable medium, who had, however, the rather unenviable reputation of being a black magician—the "Dhyan" of my article, "A Deva Revelation," published in the *Occult Review* for August, 1922. In his company I had many astral adventures— after a break in consciousness I would find myself with him upon the astral plane—but I could no longer leave my body at will. And there I met and conversed with the group of spiritual beings who manifested through my friend. Their teachings were extraordinary, and their spiritual grade seemed very high. They told me they had sealed my "Door" because I was becoming attuned to psychic forces which might sweep me away before my work on earth was done.

I can suggest another explanation which may appeal more to people who have no time for *crux ansatas* and high-grade spiritual beings. I never minded making the instantaneous projections, but it is a fact that I was always rather afraid of the Pineal Door method. You see, the sensations attending the process of getting through the "Door" were really so extremely unpleasant, though once separation was effected I had a most delightful time. The tempest over, one passed into calm and sunlit waters. As I have said, I believed that I was on the track of something "big". Therefore, when conditions permitted, I was impelled to continue my research and force this mysterious "Door"; but I did so with much the same feelings as one experiences when approaching the dentist's chair. This repressed fear may have become stored up in my unconscious mind and, reinforced by the Extension fear of my childhood, set up an inhibition, manifesting as the auto-hypnotic suggestion that I had lost my power and could no longer obtain separation by the dreaded Pineal Door method. The loss of my power would therefore be an unconscious wish fulfilment. In the same way, during the War, there were many cases where the repressed desire to escape produced blindness or paralysis and thus saved the soldier from being sent back to the front.

Nevertheless, as far as the conscious part of me is concerned, I have always greatly regretted that this method of projection is no longer possible for me, and I still live in hopes of recovering it one day. I have heard that if a projectionist once loses his power he can never regain it, but anyhow, this is only partly true in my own case.

In 1915 the Army people had refused my services ; but in March, 1917, they changed their minds and kindly entrusted me with a pick and shovel—later, a rifle also. Through two and a half years of Active Service my black *crux ansata* kept me company, and I remained a prisoner in my body. It seems the gods have a sense of humour ; for when I was invalided home after a most serious operation, the scar upon my abdomen was roughly in the shape of the Egyptian ankh. The visionary symbol still remains before my inner eyes, but it is now very faint and difficult to see. I felt none too happy at Cologne on the eve of this operation, which was for a gangrenous appendix and peritonitis. My chief concern, of course, was for my wife, but there were minor regrets also.

I felt tolerably certain that if I "went west" I should only find myself in a condition with which I was already quite familiar, but my "great discovery" would never be given to an unappreciative world. I thought of my note-books and the hopes of my College days, and I got a sense of "waste", which hurt rather. Yes, if I did pull through, I must procrastinate no longer. Something would really have to be done about things.

When I left the Army in October, 1919, I was still very keen on all matters appertaining to the Occult, but I no longer wanted to turn out stories for the magazines. I sold eight in the course of the next two years and then stopped writing them. Early in 1920 I got a job as a temporary Civil Servant, subsequently passing the first Lytton examination and becoming duly established. So now the reader will doubtless picture me twiddling my thumbs, reading the paper, doing cross-words and making tea. But alas, this is not true ! And really I get through quite a reasonable amount of work in the course of the day, what with speeding-up and "averages", and there's small time to indulge in thumb-twiddling—even if I wanted to.

It was easy to shed my khaki and get my ancient clothes on ; but not so easy to take up the threads of civilian life again. For several months the world to which I had returned seemed strange. I felt so rough and awkward and slightly dazed. Then, when I had settled down a bit, remembering a certain evening at Cologne, I got out my note-books, wrote "The Pineal Doorway", and sent it to the Hon. Ralph Shirley, Founder and Editor of the *Occult Review*. In a few days I received the proofs, and the article appeared in April, 1920. "Beyond the Pineal Door" followed in the next number, and a third article, "Dream Travelling", was published in December, 1923.

Today these articles seem only a slight contribution to the literature of the subject, but seemingly, despite my procrastination, I was first in the field in England ; for in the Editorial to the *Occult Review* for April, 1929, I find this statement : "Practically the only detailed and first-hand accounts of voluntary projection of the double hitherto available in the English language were those of Oliver Fox . . ." The first book on projection was Mr. Sylvan J. Muldoon's *The Projection of the Astral Body*, published by Messrs. Rider & Co. in 1929. Perhaps I should explain here that I do not propose to give any account of the methods of other projectionists or to compare their experiences with mine, not because I do not appreciate their work, but because this has been done already—and far more ably than I could do it— by Mr. Shirley in his *The Mystery of the Human Double*, to which reference was made in my opening chapter.

Since I lost my power to force the Pineal Door, my position has become much what it was in the early days of my research : that is, I have to depend upon either the Dream of Knowledge or the False Awakening, leading to the recognition of the fact that I am in the Trance Condition. It is true that I can still induce the preliminary symptoms of the trance at will ; but it is only on very rare occasions, when conditions are exceptionally favourable, that I can get the trance deep enough to allow of an instantaneous projection. I think it may be of service to the serious student who intends to make experiments himself (or herself) if I now give some further extracts from my records.

It will be seen from the dates that all these experiences were *after* I had lost my power of passing through the "Door" and they illustrate the results which may be obtained without any very unpleasant or frightening symptoms. Perhaps an exception should be made of the second record which seems to stand in a class apart from the others. To the general reader some of these records may seem uninteresting, and perhaps very like ordinary dreams; but I would emphasize the point that they are *not* ordinary and that, even where the experience seems trivial and of little interest, it is an example of an *abnormal* state of consciousness.

April 4, 1923.   *Kingswood Road, Merton Park, S.W.*

In the early hours of the morning I found myself in the Trance Condition. Obtained separation with full consciousness, by willing myself out of my body, and was borne away by an astral current. I came to rest in a poorly furnished room lit by gas. Two girls were sitting by a table, talking together, and I noticed that they both appeared to be suffering from some skin disease. They did not see me. My stay was very brief and I was swept away again. This time I came to rest in the country, on the bank of a river, and there I met my wife. I forget how she was dressed, except that I know she was not in her night apparel. The moon was shining brightly, making the scene very beautiful and peaceful, and we walked on together by the side of the river. I explained to her that I was experimenting in projection and that in this condition I could levitate. I then decided to try to levitate with her and took her hand, but at this moment my body called me back and the trance was broken. Fairly long duration. My wife had no memory of dreaming. It was actually moonlight when I woke.

June 11, 1928.   *Worple Road, W. Wimbledon*

In a preliminary unremembered dream I got the knowledge that I was dreaming. I decided that I would experiment and was immediately swept away by some astral current. I came to rest on a stretch of sand by the sea. It was dark, foggy and very melancholy. I was perfectly conscious of my condition and that my physical body was in bed at Worple Road, Wimbledon. I walked on for a little while through the mist, noting that the conditions seemed unusually favourable. My body was not pulling me and there were no more currents. I then decided that I would try to reach a certain ruined temple in Tibet, of which my Master, Azelda, had spoken. With this end, I concentrated all my will in one big effort, expecting to rush off in some horizontal direction.

The result was absolutely unexpected. The ground collapsed beneath my feet and I was falling, with seemingly tremendous velocity, down a dark, narrow tunnel or shaft. This downward descent continued until I lost my time-sense and it seemed that I might have been falling for hours. Something in me was getting frightened, but I managed to keep calm by telling myself that I was really in bed at Wimbledon and that my Master would protect me. At last I came gently to rest. Blackness and silence ; then, as one awaking from a heavy sleep, I became progressively aware of my surroundings.

My eyes seemed hopelessly out of focus : I could see only a blur of bright colours—red and yellow predominating. I was naked and bound to an X-shaped framework in a vertical position. Something was trickling down my bare flesh. It was blood from many wounds. I was burning and smarting all over. I could not see, because my sight had been almost destroyed by red-hot irons. Now the colours were moving. They might be the robes of men or women. Every second the pain became more acute, as though an anæsthetic were wearing off. My body seemed to be a mass of wounds and burns and hopelessly mutilated. It was very difficult now not to panic, despite my affirmations that my physical body was in bed at Wimbledon, and I wondered if I might be dying.

Then I heard a man's voice speaking close to my right ear—calm, but with a horrible insistence : "*Say* thou art Theseus !"

I seemed nearly past speech, but with a great effort I replied : "I am *not* Theseus. I am Oliver Fox, the servant of Azelda !"

My words produced an effect like the explosion of a bomb. The world seemed to collapse about me : a chaos of blinding light, terrific sounds, and a whirling tempest. My return was instantaneous, and the trance was broken. I found myself trembling and my heart beating violently. It was very nice to see my wife sleeping peacefully beside me. As it was still dark, this experience must have occurred in the early hours of the morning. I tried to think just who Theseus was, but mixed him up with "Thaddeus of Warsaw". I had the idea in my mind that I might have contacted the akashic records and stumbled, as it were, upon the last episode in the life of one of the predecessors in my Group—or, in Theosophical language, upon a past incarnation of myself. And if that were so, I hoped most sincerely that there was not another death like that still ahead of me. But very soon I fell asleep again and slept dreamlessly for the rest of the night.

Note : I was a bit shaky inwardly for all the next day, but there were no bad after-effects. The fact that Theseus, slayer of the Minotaur, was one of the greatest heroes of Mythology seems to point to colossal vanity on the part of my subconscious self, and I must admit that this experience would be more convincing if the name had been a more ordinary one. There is, however, the possibility that this great name may have become fairly common at some period—even now unfortunate babies get christened Hercules !—and it might conceivably have been the actual name of some forerunner of mine who got into a political bother and was being forced to confess to his identity. It may seem strange that I could fall asleep again almost at once after a bad scare, but sometimes an overwhelming weariness will follow the return to the body. This experience had all the "feel" of a true Pineal Door projection ; and I think it is just possible that on this one occasion, despite the loss of my power, I may have passed through the "Door" while my physical self was unconscious. Presumably the memory of the preliminary Dream of Knowledge became wiped out in the tempestuous return.

November 3, 1929.   *Worple Road, W. Wimbledon*

Dreamed that my wife and I were in bed in a strange room. An electric light hung over the bed, and my wife was brightly illuminated by it. Suddenly she disappeared from my sight ; she seemed to dissolve into a cloud and vanish. This told me that I was dreaming, and I decided to experiment in prolonging the dream and to explore. The atmosphere of the dream then became subtly changed, and I experienced that wonderful sense of mental clarity and well-being which results from the abnormal state of consciousness produced by knowing, in a dream, that one is dreaming. I knew that I was functioning in my astral vehicle while my physical body was in a condition of trance at Worple Road. I then rose from the bed and took note of my strange surroundings. This bedroom was a huge apartment, panelled from floor to ceiling in red lacquer, richly ornamented with oriental scenes. The bed and all the furniture were of the same beautiful colour and workmanship. In particular, I remember an enormous wardrobe. The bed had silken sheets and an orange silk quilt and coverlet.

I passed out into a long passage, in which were many doors. One was ajar, and I saw a bathroom dimly lit by the starlight coming through a window. From a room near the end of this passage voices reached me, and I thought that I could detect a woman's. I decided that I would enter this room, but at that instant I was caught up by some astral current and borne away. I then found myself standing on a parapet on the roof of this great palace, which was built of shining white stone and very lofty. Below, I could glimpse a sea of housetops, with here and there a twinkling light. I was about to launch myself into space, when I became aware of a young man standing beside me, but I cannot remember his appearance.

He took hold of my left wrist. "Take me with you, Brother," he pleaded ; "for I cannot go by myself." I consented, though I feared it would curtail my experiment. I stepped off the parapet and by a mental effort shot forward at a great speed, bearing my companion with me.   Together we passed over the housetops.   I remember a golden glow streaming through some attic window, and once we passed close by a chimney which belched out a shower of sparks and a dense column of sooty smoke.

As I had expected, my companion's weight soon began to tell on me.   I found myself sinking, and the call of my physical body (which I knew quite well was in bed at Worple Road, Wimbledon) battled ever more strongly with my effort to prolong the dream.   Very gently we sank into a street.   I had a brief confused impression of my companion lying on the ground and of people moving about us, then I was drawn back to my body almost instantaneously and the trance was broken.

December 8, 1929.   *Worple Road, West Wimbledon*

Very early in the morning I experienced the False Awakening.   I got out of bed and tried to switch on the electric light, but it would not work.   This told me I was dreaming, and I then realized that separation had taken place and that I was actually out of my body, having left it when I got off the bed.   At this point I saw a misty form—a woman's—standing by the bed near my wife.   This form seemed to fall backwards and vanish as I drew near it.   I then launched myself out through the window into the stormy night, and I could feel myself pass through the panes of glass.   I willed to reach that ancient Tibetan temple of which my Master, Azelda, had spoken.   Keeping the password well in mind, I travelled on at a great speed in a horizontal direction. In what seemed to be a very short space of time it grew lighter, and I could see what appeared to be the half-excavated ruins of some mighty building or temple built of brown rock or stone. Then, much to my disappointment, my body called me back and the trance was broken.

Later I succeeded in getting again into the Trance Condition. I left my body by willing myself out of it and passed into the front room. It was brilliantly illuminated by a golden light, and I saw to my surprise that some of the furniture and objects were strange and very beautiful. In particular, I noticed a small oriental cabinet. The furniture on one side of the room, however, was as it really is. The fire-place appeared to have shifted into a corner. It occurred to me that these changes might possibly be produced by thought-streams impinging upon my consciousness and causing a vision. I decided that I would make another attempt to reach the temple, approaching it from the same direction as before. Crossing the landing, I returned to my bedroom, which was normal in appearance ; but just as I was going to pass through the window, my wife gave a nervous start in her sleep and jolted my physical body. This broke the trance, and my return was so rapid that it seemed almost to coincide with her movement.

February 27, 1930.   *Worple Road, West Wimbledon*

I dreamed that I was walking, by day, through some unfamiliar street containing very fine buildings. There were plenty of people about in ordinary attire. Some incident or incongruous detail, which I cannot remember, told me I was dreaming, and I decided to experiment in prolonging the dream. I just walked on, like a visitor to a strange town. I noticed that I was dressed in the uniform of an Army officer; so when I passed a very fine War Memorial, I played my part by giving it "eyes left" and saluting. I also returned the salute of a soldier who happened to pass me. The uniform was brown, but I am not sure whether it was British. Nevertheless, I had perfect consciousness of my real physical condition. I knew I was a Clerical Officer at the —— Dept. and that my body was sleeping in my home in Worple Road. I knew also that in my Army days I was only a private.

By and by I left the street and found myself in a pretty country road. The hedgerows and trees were in full leaf, and the sky blue and sunlit. I had my usual feeling (in these experiments) of wonderful health and vitality, and the atmosphere was charged with beauty and the sense of coming adventure. Very glamorous indeed; but the effort of prolonging the dream was causing a pressure in my head, and the experience had a commonplace ending. Just as I was watching two boys with a donkey coming towards me down this country road, my body suddenly called me back and the trance was broken.

Note : If an earthly place formed the scene of my out-of-the-body adventure, it was obviously in a country where the seasons are in advance of ours; but my officer's uniform, and the fact that the soldier could see me, make it appear more probable that this experience was purely astral in its setting. Was this an unconscious wish fulfilment ? No, I think not ! I have always shirked responsibility and am too much of a vagabond to hanker after the Officers' Mess.

September 7, 1930. *Worple Road, West Wimbledon*

I dreamed that I woke in the night in our bedroom at Worple Road. I had a great longing for chocolate, but knew there was none in the house. I therefore dressed, without waking my wife, and walked to the Raynes Park railway station, thinking I might get some chocolate from a machine on the platform. No one was about and I made my way there all right, but no chocolate was left in the machines. I then thought I would take a short stroll. Leaving the station, I soon came to a shop—a tea-room and confectioner's—which was open, although it was the middle of the night. At the back of this shop was a large conservatory, and there I sat down at a round marble-topped table. I then noticed, to my surprise, a dozen or more green parrots perched in the branches of some trees which were planted in tubs. The parrots regarded me inquiringly with their orange-rimmed eyes, but made no sound. At a table near by, three or four children were huddled up together fast asleep. Presently a plump, middle-aged woman came to attend to me. She had no chocolate, but some very nice nougat—if I did not mind waiting a little while as she was not quite sure where she had put it. I assented and she departed. It then occurred to me I must have been out some time and that, if my wife woke, she would wonder what had happened to me. Strangely enough I had not thought of this before.

I hurriedly left the shop and began making for home.

Then, quite suddenly, the ridiculous nature of my behaviour—going out in the middle of the night for chocolate—dawned upon me. How came I to behave so foolishly ? And that strange shop with all those wakeful silent parrots and the sleeping children—Why, of course ! No need to trouble about my wife. I was dreaming ; and now I knew it, I was free to experiment. I then decided I would try to reach my Master, Azelda. I made a great mental effort and immediately started to glide very quickly—but *backwards*. On I rushed, through buildings and over fields at an ever-increasing speed, and as I travelled in this strange fashion I was concentrating upon the Master. It did not seem to me, however, that I had been gliding long, and nothing of interest had happened, when my body called me back and I awoke, much to my disappointment.

By steady concentration I succeeded in getting back into the trance state and projected myself out of my body by a mental effort. Once again I was speeding through the night, but this time my motion was forwards. And then, unfortunately, my wife moved and touched me. This broke the trance, and I could not re-establish it.

Note : The backward motion is very interesting ; for it is the only example I have at present of travelling in this way at the beginning of a glide, though the *return* to the body very often occurs in this fashion. Indeed, it strongly suggests that, though the scene of my adventure seemed to be quite close to my home, it was really an astral experience and that my body was calling me back from the time when I attempted to reach my Master. Thus, when I thought I was starting out on a fresh journey, I was really being drawn back. My dream of waking was, I think, the False Awakening that denotes the Trance Condition. Separation was effected when I got up to dress, but I was not conscious of my out-of-the-body state. Probably I actually visited the Raynes Park station; for the Worple Road and station seemed quite normal. Later a change of vibration appears to have taken place, and when I entered that fantastic shop, which had no physical counterpart to my knowledge, the experience became definitely astral in nature.

September 13, 1931. *Worple Road, West Wimbledon*

I dreamed that I woke in the daylight, got out of bed, and walked across the landing into our sitting-room. I looked out into the Worple Road. All the details of the street and room were very real and vivid, especially the new blue wallpaper and the pictures and china. I then noted a discrepancy: an oriental lacquer cabinet stood near the little table bearing our miniature Chinese gardens. We have no cabinet, and this told me I was dreaming. I then walked back to the bedroom and saw my wife lying in bed and seemingly awake. I told her we were dreaming and kissed her. This terminated the dream and I awoke. It was actually daylight, but my wife was asleep.

Note : Another example of the False Awakening. Separation was probably effected when I dreamed that I got out of bed. Even when I knew I was dreaming, I was not fully conscious of my out-of-the-body condition, for it did not occur to me to experiment further by leaving the house.   Kissing my wife was a mistake ; for the emotion aroused interrupted my mental control and broke the trance.

November 17, 1931.   *Worple Road, West Wimbledon*

In some way, which I cannot recall, I got the know-ledge that I was dreaming and then experimented in prolonging the dream.   It was daylight, and I found myself walking through a narrow street with shops on either side.   Presently I came to some fields which I crossed.   These led to a hill, and this I climbed and descended.   I then saw that I was on the outskirts of a town which the hill had hidden.   The shops were open and people were about.   I noticed a milkman's horse and cart.   Just as I was passing a butcher's shop, my body called me back and the experiment ended.   Unfortunately I did not note the names above the shops, but the dress of the people seemed to be quite ordinary.

Note : I was fully conscious that my physical body was asleep at Worple Road, and the experience had the peculiar glamour and vividness I have so often described ; but in the return journey, which seemed practically instantaneous, my memories had become blurred.   As it was still dark when I awoke, this experience must have been either purely astral or in some earthly place ahead of us in time.

November 27, 1932.   *Rothesay Avenue, Merton Park,*
                                                                *S.W.*20

In the night I experienced the False Awakening and thought that I was talking to my wife.   Though I was in a state of trance with very painful symptoms—great pressure in the head and seeming muscular rigidity—I did not realize my true condition. Even when two women, one dark and the other fair, entered our bedroom and began talking to us I still did not realize that they were illusions from the physical standpoint, but I was surprised by their unexpected intrusion. At this point I experienced a sudden transition to a brilliantly lighted ballroom where many people were dancing. I knew that a moment before I had been in the bedroom at Rothesay Avenue and this, together with the memory of the pains and the two women, told me that I was really functioning outside of my physical body. I was swept out of the ballroom by some current and borne away to further adventures, but the memory of these was lost in the return journey.

May 17, 1936. Rothesay Avenue, Merton Park, S.W.20

After an early cup of tea I dozed off again and presently became aware that I was in the Trance Condition. I then succeeded in leaving my body by willing myself out of it. I was borne away at great speed and came to rest in some country road. I walked along for perhaps a couple of hundred yards and came to a horse feeding on some grass by the roadside. I stroked it and could distinctly feel its warm, rather rough coat, but it did not seem aware of my presence. This, however, was a mistake ; for it distracted my attention from the experiment, and my body called me back. The duration of this experience was therefore only short.

March 1, 1938. Rothesay Avenue, Merton Park, S.W.20

Dreamed that I was walking in a strange street at night. Some incident or observation, which I cannot recall, gave me the knowledge that I was dreaming. Decided to experiment. The conditions were unusually favourable for levitation. I rose quite easily to a height of several hundred feet (an exceptional height to reach, as I was not skrying) and then glided horizontally with increasing velocity. Passed from night to day, witnessing a glorious sunrise. The horizontal motion gradually slowed down and I found myself floating high above some town. I passed a railway station with a name something like Ipswich, but obviously it could not have been our Ipswich. I decided to descend and explore. Came down gently in a little public garden or park and saw a bed of blue lobelia. It seemed to be summer in this place and also early in the morning, for few people were about and they took no notice of me. I walked down a street of quaint buildings ; the shops were not yet open.

Presently I came to a lake in front of a picturesque old house. I noticed a woman looking out of a window, and some ducks swimming on the lake. The water had overflowed and flooded a narrow tree-lined lane. I walked a short distance up this lane, but could not feel the water though it was half-way to my knees, and then my body called me back. The return was almost instantaneous. This was a most enjoyable experience : very glamorous. I was perfectly conscious all the time of my identity, that my body was in bed at Rothesay Avenue, etc. The seeming duration would be about twenty minutes.

CHAPTER IX

THE TWO WAYS OF APPROACH : SOME
PRACTICAL HINTS

I HAVE now reached a point in my narrative where a recapitulation of the symptoms and phenomena attending my two methods of attaining separation may be attempted. I am afraid a certain amount of repetition, which may, perhaps, be a little tedious to the general reader, is unavoidable ; but this chapter is intended primarily for the student who means to experiment for himself, and I hope that it may prove helpful to him. It is essentially a subtle subject, and it is difficult to convey by the written word the *reality* of the result obtained. Indeed, I have found to my surprise that some people, quite intelligent in many ways, seem fundamentally incapable of grasping the ideas I have sought to convey. To them, there are only two states of consciousness : waking and sleeping. A dream is just a dream and can't be anything else—and there you are ! Further progress is rendered impossible by this attitude. And this is my justification for rather labouring the points in my notes to some of the records which I have given and in my present summing up of the phenomena.

It would now be well to consider what risks, if any, are involved in the making of such experiments. Here

I do not feel on very sure ground ; for though I *do* know that some of the symptoms attending the Pineal Door method are painful and extremely unpleasant, I have no evidence that they are really as dangerous as they feel or injurious to the health of the experimenter. I think, however, this much can be said with certainty : no one with a weak heart should seek practical acquaintance with the phenomena of separation ; and very excitable, nervous people would do well to leave the subject alone. We are dealing with what is essentially a *mental* exercise or process, and it is easily conceivable that an ill-balanced mind, lacking in self-control, might become temporarily or even permanently deranged.

Possible dangers, including those of an occult description, may be enumerated as follows :

(1) Heart failure, or insanity, arising from shock.

(2) Premature burial. (See Chapter III.)

(3) Temporary derangement caused by the non-coincidence of the *etheric* body with the physical body after the experiment. This might render the experimenter temporarily incapable of distinguishing between waking life and dream-life. Though actually awake, he would act as one does in dreams and so appear mentally deranged—as indeed he would be for the time being. In the case of a person with an unusually "loose" etheric vehicle, such an effect may be produced by a purely involuntary extrusion of the etheric double during sleep or in the drowsy condition which preludes it.

(4) Cerebral hæmorrhage. I have been told that a too intense concentration may lead to the bursting of a blood-vessel in the brain.

(5) Severance of the Cord, which means "death".

(6) Repercussion effects upon the physical vehicle caused by injuries to the astral. Such results are extremely rare and are similar to stigmata phenomena and the production of birthmarks by cravings and frights.

(7) Obsession. I do not think we should dismiss this possibility too lightly, especially in the case of a person of known mediumistic tendencies. Although I have had no experience of it myself, I should not be surprised if this danger was a very real one.

It seems a formidable list, and I have thought it advisable to give it ; but I would not dissuade any earnest investigator with a passion for truth. He will be protected, I believe, by the unseen intelligences that guide our blundering efforts in the divine quest, and the merely frivolous inquirer will soon be frightened away by the strange initial experiences. Very likely these experiments are no more dangerous than motoring ; but I must confess that I do not really understand what I have been doing. It is easy to say, "The Soul leaves the body and returns to it" ; but this riddle of projection—of what actually happens—is in truth a most profound subject and hedged around with many subtle problems.

I hope it will be clear by now that there are two roads open to the would-be projectionist : the Way of Dreams and the Way of Self-induced Trance, i.e. either a dream or waking life may be his starting-point· There is little to choose as regards difficulty between the two methods of approach ; but the first is undoubtedly more pleasant and it may also be less dangerous.

I would advise the "dreamers of strange dreams", who are able to remember their nocturnal wanderings, to try this method first.

Some people would have us believe they never dream—except for a nightmare after an unwise supper —but it is difficult to credit this statement. They do not *remember* their dreams, probably because the subject has no interest for them. I suspect, too, that often a repressed fear of the Unknown is at the root of their inability to remember—another case of the unconscious wish fulfilment. But this much may be said : the more interest we take in our dreams, the more easily shall we remember them.

A counsel of perfection is to note the dream immediately upon waking ; but for people who have to rise early and go to work, this method possesses the serious disadvantage of breaking the night's rest rather badly. However, it is well to have pencil and paper by one's bed, ready to note anything of really exceptional interest before going to sleep again ; for it is the only *sure* method of preserving the experience. A very good plan is to make a mental *précis* of the dream, noting the salient points or stages by perhaps a single word, and then memorizing this chain of words before going to sleep again. With practice the process does not take long and is not nearly so disturbing as sitting up and switching on the light, etc.

Sometimes we may be unlucky and unable to recall our "clues", but generally we shall remember the salient points they represented, even if much of the associated detail be lost. People who find it difficult to recall their dreams should note every fragment they can bring through—however slight or absurd—for the act of noting dreams certainly stimulates the ability to remember them. Also, events may prove that what would appear to the unitiated of no importance may possess great significance. The fact that the long sides of the paving-stones were parallel to the kerb would make little difference to a picture of a street-scene, yet observing this in a dream was fraught with surprising consequences for me.

Having acquired some facility in remembering dreams—with the result that dreams now appear to increase in frequency—the next step is to awaken the critical faculty (normally dormant in dreams) and by noting some incongruous happening, or anachronism, or inconsistent detail, to obtain the knowledge (in the dream) that one is dreaming. Degrees of awareness and the phenomena attending the Dream of Knowledge —the exquisite sense of freedom, well-being, mental clarity, extended powers, gliding, levitation, etc.—have been described in Chapter III and in some of my records.

The student will find that the mental strain of prolonging the dream induces these curious sensations : his feet feel heavier and heavier, he moves as though struggling against the pull of an increasingly powerful elastic cord which seems to be attached between the shoulder-blades, and finally he develops a pain—dull at first, but swiftly becoming more acute—in the top of the head and the centre of the forehead.

On feeling this warning pain, he should terminate the experiment by ceasing his resistance and willing to awake. He will then have the sensation of being drawn backwards at an amazing speed by this elastic cord which appears to link him with his physical body. He should then be able to break the trance quite easily and experience no unpleasant symptoms.

I think that in some cases ignoring this warning pain might be very dangerous. If, however, the intrepid (or foolhardy) experimenter decides to continue prolonging the dream in defiance of the pain, which I definitely do not advise, he will probably experience a phase of dual consciousness, lose the pain, hear a "click" in his brain, and find it very difficult to end the dream and wake.

On returning to his body he will find it in a cataleptic state, and I now think the best thing he can do is just to go to sleep again instead of struggling to break the trance. His body will in all probability be normal when he wakes. This advice should be borne in mind ; for I have heard of several cases where a person has awakened in this condition and been greatly distressed, knowing nothing of projection and fearing he had become paralysed.

When the student has succeeded in obtaining a few Dreams of Knowledge, it will probably not be long before he makes acquaintance with the False Awakening. He will believe himself to be awake—though feeling strangely disinclined to move—until that curious sense of atmospheric tension, the peculiar sounds (see Chapter V), invisible hands touching him, or perhaps even an apparition, all combine to tell him that he is *not* awake but in the Trance Condition. If he does not like this experience, he can easily end it by moving and breaking the trance, which is usually quite

light in the False Awakening ; but when he has grown
accustomed to this state, the time is ripe for essaying a
conscious projection.

Let him first try to sit up *out of his body* : that is,
he will not try to move his physical body by any muscular effort, but make a purely mental attempt. Unless
it happens to be one of those cases where the Pineal
Door has been passed while the student was unconscious, he will certainly fail and nothing will happen.
Let him now concentrate all his will-power on the idea
of jumping out of, or hurling himself from, his body,
and in all probability he will succeed in making his
first Instantaneous projection. He will find himself
passing in a flash through the walls of the house ; and
after that almost anything may seem to happen to
him until something occurs to break the trance. There
will be no difficulty about coming back, for he will
return to his body as quickly as he departed from it,
and his condition should become normal almost immediately.

Of course, when the student has learnt to recognize
the Trance Condition he can always attempt a Pineal
Door projection, once he has assured himself by the
failure of the gentle "sitting up" test that the "Door"
has not already been passed.

I have said that the Way of Dreams is a more
pleasant road and probably less dangerous, but it has
two disadvantages : (1) opportunities for experiment
are limited to the comparatively rare occasions when
one is able to achieve the Dream of Knowledge or
happens to find oneself in the Trance Condition with
the preliminary work, as it were, already done ; (2) as a

rule—though by no means invariably—the experience is a little inferior in quality, just a shade less vivid, and one has very little control over one's movements, being almost completely at the mercy of those mysterious astral currents.   Nevertheless, as I hope my records will have shown, the Instantaneous method is by no means to be despised.   It is in any case a remarkable experience, well worth all the preliminary efforts, and it may lead to very surprising results.

Let us now consider the Way of Self-induced Trance, where our starting-point is not from a dream but from waking life.   I am afraid this is the only way for people who can make no progress in remembering their dreams.   Briefly stated, the problem before the experimenter is this : to send the *body* to sleep while the mind is kept *awake*.   Favourable times to experiment are after a substantial repast or when we wake in the morning feeling very loath to arise; for the body is then naturally disposed to enter the trance state.   Speaking for myself, it does not matter whether I lie on my back or on my side ; and some of my best results have been obtained in the latter position, despite the fact that one projectionist has stated that separation can be effected only when lying on one's back.

Having chosen his position, the student should concentrate upon an imaginary trap-door within his brain. His breathing should be deep and rhythmical, his eyes closed, but rolled upwards and slightly squinting. Presently he will feel a numbness, starting at his feet and travelling up his legs until eventually it spreads all over the body.   This numbness deepens into a sensation of muscular rigidity, which may become quite painful, especially in the muscles of the jaw, and there is a feeling of great pressure in the head. At this stage he will have the effect of being able to see through his closed eyelids, and the room will appear to be illuminated by a pale golden radiance. There may also be flashes of light, apparitions, and (almost certainly) terrifying noises. He may also have the illusion that someone is trying to wake him or dissuade him from making the adventure. He should tell himself that such apparitions are subject to his will and powerless to harm him ; and he should disregard any interrupting influence—even if it seems to proceed from his wife ! —for I think it is practically a certainty that if any person were really there and trying to wake him, the trance would be broken at once.

And now the student will be experiencing the very peculiar sensation of having *two* bodies : the painful physical one and, imprisoned within it, a fluidic body. He is ready for the next step, which is, by a supreme effort of the will, to force this subtle vehicle through the imaginary trap-door in his brain. It will seem to him that his incorporeal self, which was coincident with its physical prison, now rushes up his body and becomes condensed in that pineal point within his brain and batters against the door, while the pale golden light increases to a blaze of glory and a veritable inferno of strange sounds assails his ears. If the attempt should fail, the sensations are reversed. The incorporeal self subsides and becomes again coincident with the physical body, while the light dies down and the sounds diminish in violence.

If the attempt succeeds, he will have the extraordinary

sensation of passing through the door in his brain and
hearing it "click" behind him ; but he will *not* seem to
be out of his body yet.   It will appear to him that his
fluidic self has again subsided within his physical body ;
but the terrifying sounds and apparitions are no more,
and the room is evenly illuminated by the pale golden
radiance.   There is a blessed sense of calm after storm,
and fear gives place to triumphant exaltation ; for
the phase of terror, with its suggestions of coming
death or madness, is over.   He has passed through the
Pineal Door.   If the first attempt should fail, it is well
to strengthen the trance by continuing the concentration
for a little while before making the next.

Out student will still feel himself to be within his
physical body ; but now he can get out of bed in leisurely
fashion and walk away, *leaving his entranced body behind him on the bed.*   He may be able to see it, judging
from the evidence of other projectionists, but I could
not see mine.   The experience is so extremely real that
he may wonder if he is walking in his sleep—if he
cannot see his body upon the bed.   His doubts will
speedily be set at rest when he finds he can walk
through the wall.   He will undoubtedly have the dual
consciousness I have described so often while near his
body, but this sensation will be completely lost on
leaving the room or house.   Should he feel nervous at
this first venture, it might be well not to leave the room,
but to sit in a chair—which will support him all right so
long as he believes it will—and just think things over.
He can open the door—but not of course the real
physical door—or he can just walk through it without
seeming to open it.   He can pass through the wall ; but

if he doubts his ability to do this, he will probably find
that it stops him as it would in waking life.

Once outside the house—and especially if he has no
pre-arranged plan of action—the chances are that he
will find himself caught up by some invisible force and
borne away, flashing through houses, trees, etc., until
he finally comes to rest in some totally unexpected
place. Sometimes the speed seems so tremendous
that one gets the effect of tumbling through a hole into
a new sphere. There is nothing to be afraid of and *no
warning pain.* I believe it is quite safe to stay out as
long as one can ; for sooner or later the experience will
be terminated by some force outside one's control. I
have seen the body I travel in (etheric, astral, or perhaps
mental) seemingly clothed in many ways, but never
naked—except in the last phase of the Theseus adventure, and then I only *felt* that I was naked as I was nearly
blind. Occasionally I have not been able to see any
astral body when I looked for it—no legs, no arms, no
body !—an extraordinary sensation—just a *consciousness*, a man invisible even to himself, passing through
busy streets or whizzing through space.

There is one thing that is sure to trouble the student
sooner or later in his out-of-the-body excursions : he
will lose his time-sense more or less completely. He will
be quite aware of his identity and have a perfect
memory of the events of the day up to the time of
making his experiment ; he will know well enough
that his physical body is at home in bed ; but he will
not know how long he has been out, how long the
experiment has really lasted. If the setting seems to be
purely astral in nature, there is no way of telling ; but

if the scene of his adventure seems to be on the earth, and there is no perplexing change from night to day or *vice versa*, the appearance of the sky and the position of the moon, stars, or sun will form a fairly reliable guide as to the duration of the trance.

As to his powers of locomotion, he can walk, glide, levitate and then glide at a great height, or try his luck at skrying—which, I repeat, is dangerous. In short, he can behave as an ordinary man, if it please him, or as a superman as far as the astral currents will permit. If the experiment is terminated involuntarily, he will just flash home and find himself within his body almost instantly. Generally the trance will be broken at once; but at times there may be a touch of catalepsy, and perhaps the illusion that someone is distressed and trying to restore him. If the return is voluntary—accomplished by walking home or willing himself back—the approach to the body should be quite gentle. He can walk up to the bed and lie down, and he will feel himself merge into his body and become one with it—a strange sensation. The trance will probably not be broken when the return is gentle. He can either strengthen it by further concentration, and then step out of his body again for fresh adventures, or he can break the trance by willing to awake. Once the Pineal Door has been passed, it is not necessary to pass through it again—and I believe it would be impossible to do so—as long as the trance remains unbroken.

I strongly advise the really keen student to take no chances with his memory, but to switch on the light and write his record straight away; for if he waits till morning much detail will have faded or become smoothed out or blurred—whatever the process may be—especially if he has a few more dreams before rising. As I have said, for some reason beyond my ken these memories of the discarnate experiences are peculiarly evanescent, even more fleeting than ordinary dreams. He will feel that it is quite safe to leave the recording till the morning, but it is not. And at the risk of appearing wearisome I will repeat once more : the projectionist's motto should be, "I may look, but I must not get too interested—let alone touch !" The fact that it is really very funny for me to be advising people not to procrastinate or be too—let us say—inquisitive does not affect the wisdom of my words.

I believe the art of *conscious* projection to be purely mental. From beginning to end the Will must be master, and when it loses its control the experiment is brought to a seemingly premature conclusion. Perhaps this is not so evident in my "Locked out" adventure, when I was unable for a time to terminate the out-of-the-body experience, yet even then it was through the exercise of will-power that I managed at last to return. But let it be understood that I do not claim to possess exceptional will-power. I'm afraid I have been too lazy and easy-going. Occasionally in my astral journeys I can get where I want to ; but as a rule I cannot—the currents are too strong for me—so on the whole my records make poor reading.

The reader with no practical experience of projection, even if he be kind enough not to doubt my veracity, may incline to the view that my methods lead only to a new state of consciousness, that the projection is only *seeming*, and that the question whether man possesses a soul or spirit, capable of functioning apart from his body, remains unanswered. Nor have I the least objection to his adopting this attitude. But let him follow my methods and achieve two or three successful Pineal Door projections, or even some of the Instantaneous kind, and I think he will be convinced that he has a soul and that it does leave the body in these experiments. Though I have stated the alternative view once or twice in this book, I am not sitting on the fence. I come down definitely on the side of projection ; but it is only fair to add that my belief has been greatly strengthened by the "Elsie" experience and my researches in other occult directions.

Yes, I have a soul. I have left my body many times, being fully conscious of my duality. I can still do it by the Instantaneous method when conditions permit ; but please do not ask me to give a test demonstration ! I might perhaps have done this before I lost my power, but now I cannot. I will return to this subject later on.

CHAPTER X

IT is certain that a new state of consciousness results from the methods I have employed, and I have said I believe my soul really does leave my body, but I have also confessed that I do not understand the true nature of my *modus operandi*. I have made experiments and (sometimes) noted the results, but I feel a far better brain than mine is needed to tackle the extremely obscure problems involved and formulate a satisfactory explanation of the underlying mental or spiritual process. I try to write clearly ; yet when I get away from my records and attempt to elaborate thereon, I realize the job is much too big for me. I hope that I have done some useful spade-work and helped to lay the foundations, but the building of the house I leave to others. So if this chapter induces in the reader a fogged feeling, it is fully shared by the author.

The various examples I have given in the course of this narrative show that separation may be obtained by either the Instantaneous method or the Pineal Door method, and we may now attempt a further classification :—

(1) Projection made from the Dream of Knowledge.

Sometimes this appears to be similar in nature to a true Pineal Door projection, but the consciousness has no memory of having passed through the "Door".

(2) Projection made after the False Awakening has led the experimenter to realize that he is in the Trance Condition. This may be either an Instantaneous projection, or a gentle separation—the Pineal Door, it would seem, having been passed while the experimenter was unconscious.

(3) The experimenter is lucky enough to find himself in the Trance Condition straight away and has no memory of any preliminary Dream of Knowledge or of a False Awakening. Separation may be either Instantaneous, or gentle (see above), or (if the "Door" has not already been passed) a true Pineal Door projection may be attempted.

(4) Instantaneous projection made when in a state of self-induced trance; no preliminary dream, and no break in consciousness.

(5) As (4), but a Pineal Door projection. This is the most difficult to achieve.

And now to note some, but by no means all, of the problems that suggest themselves to me.

PROBLEM I. Can a *conscious* projection be made from waking life without the Trance Condition?

I have italicized "conscious", because it would appear from cases cited by Mr. Shirley and other authorities that unconscious projections have been made without any degree of trance being manifest in the person whose double was seen. It may be, however, that in these cases a telepathic explanation is the more likely. In the early days of my research I should have said the answer to Problem 1 was definitely "No"; but now I am afraid to be dogmatic for the following reason:

My very good friend, Mr. G. Murray Nash (Paul Black), was walking home from the office in daylight through the busy street. Suddenly all the houses and people vanished. He was standing in beautiful open country. He walked on for a few yards and came to a flight of old stone steps leading down to the bank of a wide stream or little river. A boat of beautiful, but very ancient, design was moored there. Across the stern a rich purple robe had been carelessly thrown. Not a person was in sight anywhere. Mr. Nash was about to descend the steps, when the vision faded and he found himself walking on through the familiar street, and seemingly he had never stopped walking. This experience seemed to him to last for two or three minutes; but judging from his position on returning to normal consciousness, he had not walked more than half a dozen paces along the street.

Such an excursion is, of course, extremely rare and is very probably different in nature from the projections I have made. It is more like a projection into the Past and recalls the famous Versailles adventure. And that reminds me: I have been told it is possible to travel from here to, let us say, China, without astral projection, as understood in this book, being involved. There is another method which might be colloquially described as "falling through a hole in oneself into the Fourth Dimension". Needless to say, I do not understand how this is done, nor have I succeeded in doing it; but it has bearing on those strange cases of people "taken by the fairies".

PROBLEM 2. Does the Dream of Knowledge induce the Trance Condition ? or is the awakening of the normally dormant critical faculty in a dream possible *only* when, for some unknown reason, the sleeping physical body has become *abnormally* entranced ?

If the former alternative be true, the Dream of Knowledge is the real starting point of the projection experiment ; but if the latter be true, then the Dream of Knowledge is only a device which enables us to become aware that the physical body is in this unusually deep trance state.

It will be remembered, from the example I gave of the dream-lady with four eyes, that degrees of awareness are met with in dreams, so that one may hesitate upon the very brink of achieving the Dream of Knowledge and then fail.   In the ordinary way no attention is paid to the physical body in a dream, because the dreamer is not aware that the body in which he seems to be functioning is not his earthly body ; and it looks as though this awakening of the critical faculty in the dream was necessary to draw our attention to the physical body and so bring home to us our seeming duality, to make us realize that we are "out".   Scientists of the broad-minded type now hesitate to affirm that memory is merely a function of the physical brain, and I think it is pretty certain that the true seat of the critical faculty—allied as it is with the principle in us which asserts "I *am* I.   I *exist*"—is also not to be found within the brain matter.   The realization of duality causes the Soul (to put it very roughly) to withdraw to an unusual extent from the sleeping body, and so the normal sleep-condition of the latter deepens into trance.

We have seen also that even in the out-of-the-body adventures degrees of awareness are still manifest ; and the more perfect the realization of our duality, the deeper the trance. We can also dispense with the Dream of Knowledge and still obtain separation, but how do we do it ? By starting with the critical faculty *awake* and concentrating upon this idea of *duality*, and the result is that the body becomes entranced. I therefore think the Dream of Knowledge does induce the Trance Condition.

PROBLEM 3. What is the Warning Pain ?

At first one is inclined to think it merely a celestial headache caused by the strain of concentrating on prolonging the dream, or that it results from blood-pressure and congestion in the physical brain ; yet if this concentration be persisted in, the pain suddenly ceases. Why ? It may be helpful to recall that when separation has been effected by the Pineal Door method the Warning Pain is not experienced. Also, while the pain is felt, dual consciousness is operative, and the projectionist swings as it were between the dream-scene and his bedroom. The consciousness seems to be split, functioning simultaneously outside of and in the body. The seeming two halves are engaged in a battle, and I would suggest that the Warning Pain results from this conflict. The psycho-analyst might consider this phenomenon a true, though evanescent, manifestation of split personality : a struggle between the Conscious Will and the Unconscious, the latter being charged with all the repressed fears of the Unknown.

PROBLEM 4. What is the "click ?"

I cannot answer this question. The cause might be

found within the physical brain, or it might be purely psychic. Considered as a "sound" it is an illusion—similar to the noise-effects produced by blood-pressure. I heard it when I fought the Warning Pain and got "locked out" in my dream, and I have frequently experienced it at the moment of passing through the Pineal Door, though sometimes I have failed to note it —perhaps because my attention was focused upon other happenings. I have heard it also when breaking a trance of exceptional severity. As a rule it is not noticed when making an Instantaneous projection, but there have been some exceptions when I was trying a very difficult method which I have not mentioned so far. In the drowsy state that preludes sleep a mental image is formed of a well-known street or strip of country or room. The Will is then concentrated upon the idea of projecting oneself into this picture. When successful, the thing happens in a flash : the "click" is heard, and one is *there*. A moment before, the picture was *in* the consciousness ; a moment later—after the "click"—the consciousness appears to function in the picture which now forms the surrounding world. The experience is very vivid, but extremely short-lived. On the three or four occasions when I have succeeded, I did not notice the "click" on the return journey to my body, which seemed practically instantaneous. It would seem, then, that this mysterious "click" may be heard when the consciousness switches from one state to another, or when a sudden change occurs in the range of vibrations to which the soul is capable of responding ; but further than this I cannot go.

PROBLEM 5. Why did I experience such great difficulty

in ending the dream and returning to my body on the two occasions when I fought the Warning Pain until it ceased ?

I do not know, nor can I hazard a guess. It seemed like a breakdown of the Will ; yet as a rule, as soon as the mental control is lost the experiment is brought to an abrupt end. It was a complete reversal of the ordinary course of events and rather suggests the inexperienced magician who becomes the prey of the phantom he has evoked. Several times I have been tempted to get "locked out" again, and I have resisted the pain up to a certain point ; but when the crisis seemed to be very near, prudence (or cowardice ?) has prevailed.

PROBLEM 6. Are the cataleptic symptoms real—i.e. physical—or only imaginary ?

Judging from my own experiences, and bearing in mind the well-known fact that catalepsy is easily induced under hypnosis, I think there is no doubt that these symptoms are real.

PROBLEM 7. What is the true nature of the mental process which I have termed "passing through the Pineal Door ?"

From the standpoint of Psychical Research, I can only suggest that the concentration produces a temporary split in the personality ; but with the aid of Theosophy I can get a little further. The effect of turning one's attention inward upon the pineal gland is to stimulate the chakras and increase their revolutions, thus inducing clairvoyance and clairaudience—hence the visual and auditory illusions of the Trance Condition—until, as a culmination, the consciousness becomes identified to some degree, albeit only very slightly and very imperfectly, with the Great Lotus of a Thousand-and-One Petals which we are told is situated just *above* the head, being therefore actually *outside* the physical body. It might therefore seem to the consciousness that it had left the body and was functioning apart from it. It must be clearly understood that in my case only the first faint stirrings of the Lotus would be involved. To have it fully operative one would have to be either a Master or a very high Adept. There may also be some connection with the Raja Yoga practice of awakening the Kundalini Serpent, coiled up in the sacral plexus, and causing it to ascend the Sushumna, which is a canal running through the centre of the spinal column.

Aleister Crowley tells us in "The Temple of Solomon the King" (*The Equinox*, Vol. I, No. 4) :

"When the Kundalini is aroused, and enters the canal of the Sushumna, all the perceptions are in the mental space or Chittakasa. When it has reached that end of the canal which opens out into the brain the objectless perception is in the knowledge space or Chidakasa."

These are just suggestions which may, or may not, have significance, and they are not made in any dogmatic spirit ; for, as I have said, I do not pretend to know what is the essential truth beneath my Pineal Door imagery. From my standpoint it does not matter if the student is a materialist and flatly refuses to believe that he has a soul, and considers his pineal gland to be merely a useless relic of some far-distant past. By doing certain things certain results will follow, and if he perseveres with my method he will at least succeed in demonstrating for his own satisfaction that a temporary phase of split personality may be induced at will. While, naturally, I am not prepared to put myself wholly under the microscope, I have tried to give the psycho-analyst a fair amount of material to work upon, should he seek to attempt a Freudian explanation of my projection experiences. And for this reason I have admitted some autobiographical matter which may have seemed not wholly pertinent to my subject. The psycho-analyst observes that a relation exists between Fact A and Fact B and then tells us that A is the cause of B ; but my view is that both A and B are effects produced by X—a factor further back still—and to find X, look to the horoscope. You see, I know that astrology *does* work, but how many students of the Freudian school would admit this ?

PROBLEM 8. What is the real difference between a Pineal Door projection and one made from the Dream of Knowledge or by the Instantaneous Method ?

Again I do not know ; but different rates of vibration, in the vehicle employed by the consciousness during its out-of-the-body adventure, may be at the root of the matter. I suggested earlier in this book that, because of this question of vibration, we must not expect to find complete agreement in the details of their seeming discarnate experiences related to us by projectionists. Beyond this vibration theory I cannot venture an opinion, but I can indicate the main differences observed by me in the results obtained by the three methods.

Dream of Knowledge Projection.

(1) The setting is as a rule more astral in nature and consequently more spectacular and varied. Greater

extremes of beauty and ugliness are encountered, and the fantastic element is more marked.

(2) I am visible to the people I encounter and can therefore talk to them. For example, in a restaurant I can order a meal and even eat, but the distracting influence on the Will soon terminates the experiment.

(3) I am at all times liable to be swept away by a current, even as a leaf is caught up by a sudden wind.

(4) When levitating, it is difficult to rise more than a hundred feet, a strong downward pull being felt.

(5) I am subject to the Warning Pain and the pull of the Cord.

(6) The degree of realization of my out-of-the-body state varies, but generally it is very vivid. Just at times the possibilities for useful experiment will be missed and I am content to take things as they come, though quite aware of my identity and that my physical body is in bed.

(7) Duration generally fairly short if the Warning Pain is obeyed. I mean, of course, the seeming duration. The time actually occupied, as measured by the clock, is another matter.

Pineal Door Projection.

(1) The effect is that I am earth-bound, a veritable pale ghost revisiting the glimpses of the moon. Except for a certain glamour, which enhances the beauty of the scenes and imparts an atmosphere of mystery and seeming vitality even to the commonplace and inanimate, the places I visit seem to be on this earth. Sometimes a change of vibration may occur, so that the experience becomes more astral in nature and the

fantastic element may intrude, but this is rare. It is strange that this very painful and difficult method should lead to such ordinary—but exceedingly *real*—surroundings.

(2) As a rule I am quite invisible to the people I meet and therefore cannot talk to them. In a restaurant I cannot order a meal, because the waiter is unaware of my presence. If I spoke to him he would not hear ; but if I touched him he would *feel* me and give such a start that the trance would be broken. However, if I do not concentrate my attention upon people, I can pass through their bodies without their becoming aware of my presence. Only very rarely have I been visible to another person and able to enter into conversation. And in these exceptional cases our talk has been of very brief duration ; for the act of speaking divided my attention and upset my mental control, and the trance was broken. In Dreams of Knowledge I have frequently encountered beings who were seemingly far above me in spiritual grade ; but I have never met with such in my fully-conscious functioning on the astral plane after forcing the Pineal Door. In all these experiments I have seemed to be peculiarly isolated, meeting no superior intelligence, nor have I come across a fellow-investigator. Once I have won through the intermediate trance state and passed the Door, I have not seen any elementals or other terrifying beings—such as the horrible creatures and freakish animals to be found in the astral hells.

(3) Although still subject to the currents, they are less frequent, and as a general rule I have far more control over the experiment.

(4) Levitation is much easier, very little or no downward pull being felt, and it is possible to rise to great heights. Indeed, a seeming height of many miles may be reached by skrying ; but, as I have said, this method differs from levitation and is very dangerous.

(5) There is no Warning Pain, and the pull of the Cord is seldom felt unless the experiment is terminated abruptly and involuntarily by some untoward happening breaking the trance. In this case the Cord—like a mighty rope of stretched elastic—seems to come into operation all at once, and I am drawn backwards with tremendous speed, re-entering my body with the effect of "a bang".

(6) The degree of realization of the out-of-the-body state does not vary and is really perfect. The Pineal Door method scores heavily here. And the same applies to that wonderful feeling of well-being and mental clarity which my readers are probably tired of hearing about by now. Alas, that words should be so futile !

(7) Duration : here too this method is greatly superior ; for a series of excursions may be made, without breaking the original trance, by returning to the physical body, strengthening the trance by concentrating upon it, and then leaving the body again.

Instantaneous Projection.

(1) The setting may be apparently on the earth, or purely astral, or switch from one to the other.

(2) When the earthly element predominates, I am invisible to people ; but when the experience is more astral in nature, I am visible to people and can therefore converse with them.

(3) Astral currents at their strongest. As a rule I have very little power to influence the course of events. Even worse, from the "control" standpoint, than the Dream of Knowledge projection.

(4) Levitation conditions much the same as in the Dream of Knowledge projection. Perhaps slightly better.

(5) As in the Dream of Knowledge projection ; but owing to the short duration of the average experiment, the Warning Pain and the pull of the Cord are not often experienced. Dual consciousness also is rare in projections of this kind.

(6) The degree of realization of the out-of-the-body state is usually quite good, and perhaps better than in the Dream of Knowledge projection ; but it is inferior to that experienced beyond the Pineal Door.

(7) The duration is, as a rule, very brief. Occasionally, however, I have seemed to be out of my body for about twenty minutes.

It should be observed that these notes refer to conscious projections. As will be seen from some of my records, the actual separation may be made during a period of unconsciousness and be followed by the realization of the out-of-the-body state. Sometimes, too, through failing to recognize the False Awakening, it will seem to the projectionist that he is getting out of bed at the time when he leaves his body, as in my "chocolates and parrots" record.

Yram, the French projectionist, among other rather startling statements, claimed to be able to achieve a whole series of projections, passing from plane to plane and leaving a chain of bodies, or vehicles, behind him in the process. The word "chain" is mine and is, of course, misleading ; the layers in an onion provide a better simile ; but really, as I have said more than once, it is all a matter of vibration. I will make no comment on Yram's claim beyond stating that I have three—and only three—records of a very puzzling nature, which do not seem to fit in with the classification I have attempted, and which do rather suggest that a second projection was made by me on these occasions. But I do not feel at all sure about this, and I have at times thought that these three perplexing examples should really be called "Dreams of Making a Projection", or more simply, "Pseudo-Projections". I will now give these records, together with my notes made at the time, and leave the reader to judge for himself.

March 24, 1916.   *Foundry Lane, Southampton*

I dreamed that Mrs. X, Mr. J, my wife and I were talking together in Mrs. X's sitting-room where we have all met on several occasions to discuss matters arising from the mediumistic and clairvoyant gifts of Mrs. X and Mr. J. I did not know that I was dreaming. As the result of our meeting, very strong psychic forces were manifesting—which usually happens. I entranced what I thought was my physical body and obtained separation by the Pineal Door method. I then saw that the room was full of flashing astral lights and that many forms were building up. Having left my body, I passed before Mrs. X and my wife (I could not tell whether they were able to see me) and halted beside Mr. J. He certainly could see me in my astral (or mental ?) vehicle, and we remained conversing together. I do not remember what we said. Finally something occurred to break my trance, and I awoke.

Note : From the after-effects observed by me on waking, I believe that my body had actually been in the Trance Condition. I think the following explanation is probably correct—from the occult standpoint : the four of us actually met upon the astral plane. As I was not aware that I was dreaming, I naturally mistook my astral body for my physical body which was lying at home, already in the Trance Condition, though I did not know this. My attempt to entrance my astral body deepened the trance of the physical through repercussion, thus creating the illusion that separation had only then been accomplished, whereas I had really been separated from my physical body all the time. Another explanation is that I succeeded in attaining a second degree of separation and was functioning in my mental body—freed from both astral and physical vehicles—when I was talking to Mr. J ; but this theory seems to me less probable than the first.

February 23, 1930. *Worple Road, W. Wimbledon*

I dreamed that my wife and I were in a room somewhat resembling the dining-room of my old home at Forest View, Southampton. My wife was sitting in a chair on the left of the hearth, and I was on a sofa near the window. The room was nearly in darkness, so I tried to switch on the light, but it would not work. This told me that I was dreaming ; but I believed myself to be lying on the sofa in this room, and I did not realize that I was in bed at Worple Road, Wimbledon. I then made a great mental effort to leave my (astral ?) body and found myself rushing through space at a tremendous speed until I suddenly came to rest in what I felt was another sphere.

I was in a vast and lovely garden beneath an intensely blue sky. The effect was of brilliant sunlight, but I do not remember seeing the sun. Beautiful flowers abounded, and gaily-hued birds were flitting to and fro. I joined a stream of people, robed in various colours, and entered a large lecture-hall or temple. The people regarded me curiously, as though I were a stranger ; but although they made no signs of welcome, they did not seem actually to resent my presence. In this temple or hall I sat down in the front row of seats just before a raised platform. Then there appeared on the dais a thin, dark, austere-looking man robed in black. This priest, or teacher, at once singled me out and approached me.

"You do not belong here," he said—or words to that effect.

"No," I replied ; "and as my body may call me back at any moment, you may as well let me stay as long as I can."

"Do you know where you are ?" he asked.

I answered that I believed all the people around me were what the world calls "dead" and that I too might perhaps pass to this sphere when my time came. Then, before he could reply, my body called me back and my return was almost instantaneous.

Note : From my sensations, in the out-of-the-body experience and on my return to my physical vehicle, I am inclined to think that this was really a true projection. Apart from the curious fact that I had gone back in time some 23 years, to a period when my wife and I were living at Forest View, I was perfectly conscious of my condition after the failure of the electric light had told me that I was dreaming.

December 20, 1930.   *Worple Road, West Wimbledon*

I dreamed that I was at the office in the daylight. As I sat at my desk, I fell into a reverie and had a vision in which my wife was standing near some white flowers in a garden. I held the vision in my mind and was examining the flowers, when it occurred to me to try to project myself into this garden. With this end, I concentrated upon the white flowers. Then something seemed to snap in my head and instantly I found myself standing by my wife in the garden, which was flooded with bright sunshine—or a light resembling this. It was very interesting to note how all at once the white flowers had changed from a mere mental image into a seemingly solid reality. My wife was not surprised, though I must have seemed to appear quite suddenly. I explained to her my experiment and said that my body was at the office and that I supposed she must really be asleep and dreaming. Then I awoke.

Note: From my physical sensations on awaking and also the peculiar state of consciousness experienced in the dream, I think my body was actually in the trance state and that I was functioning in my astral vehicle at first, and later, perhaps, during the seeming projection, in my mental body. On rare occasions, when in the Trance Condition, I have concentrated upon a well-known scene and then succeeded in projecting myself into it. There came that queer sensation of a "click" in the brain, and then I was *there*, the transition seeming instantaneous. The fact remains, however, that in this "white flowers" experiment my consciousness was not as perfect as usual ; for I did not realize that my physical body was in bed at Worple Road. Nevertheless, for the reasons stated, I doubt if this experience can be dismissed merely as a dream within a dream, but it was of course purely astral (or mental ?) in its setting. It was still dark when I awoke and there were no white flowers in our garden. My wife had no memory of dreaming.

CHAPTER XI

WITH the shining exception of the "Elsie" projection, I must admit this book presents but little of evidential value as to the *truth* of astral projection. It does contain a large amount of evidence—verifiable, I believe, if the reader is prepared to take the trouble— that it is possible to obtain a new state of consciousness in which the soul appears to function outside of the body ; but I have been on the whole singularly unfortunate in obtaining corroborative evidence as to the reality of my own seemingly discarnate experiences. Several people have told me they woke in the night to find me standing by the bed ; but though I do not doubt their word, on each occasion I have not been able to remember anything. And when I have seemed to encounter a person during my astral functioning, either he or she has failed to remember, or it has been a stranger, so that confirmation could not be obtained.

The question now arises : Can a really satisfactory test be devised ? And the answer is : It depends upon our attitude and whether we are prepared to be moderately reasonable. If we persist in investing the Subconscious Mind, or the Superconscious Mind, with all the powers of the Almighty, obviously it is impossible to imagine how rigid scientific proof could be obtained.

Spiritualists are in just the same difficulty ; for the Subconscious Mind theory is infinitely elastic and can be stretched to cover every phenomenon of the séance room, every seeming manifestation of man's survival—however convincing to the ordinary "non-scientific" mind. Indeed, it seems to me psychical researchers must just go round and round in circles, without getting anywhere, unless they can agree to limit somewhat the all-embracing powers at present credited to the Subconscious. It may be—and I believe it *is*—true that an infinitesimal Spark of the Logos exists in every man and that *if* he could make direct contact with this Divine Flame all knowledge would be open to him ; but the Jewel is in a safe with seven locks, and not one man in a million can hope to glimpse it even once in his lifetime. Therefore, I find it easier to believe I am in touch with a Master, a celestial being on another plane of existence, apart altogether from my consciousness (whether Sub. or Super.) and that the Golden Book came from Azelda and not from the Divine Flame in the superconscious minds of Paul Black and Oliver Fox.

I refer to our five-and-a-half years' research in purely automatic writing, where the consciousness plays no part in the transmission of the script. My left hand rested on my partner's right, and Azelda's force entered at the top of my head and travelled down my left arm. P.B. felt it like a cold breeze (streaming from my fingers) upon the back of his hand, and then the pencil would start its tempestuous passage across the paper. We could talk, read, or sit with closed eyes, without interfering with the message. I refer the curious to

"The Coming of Azelda's Golden Book," by Paul Black and Oliver Fox, published in the *Occult Review* for January, 1928. Yet, despite its extraordinary subject-matter and cumulative effect, there are many people who would dismiss the 192,000 words of the Azelda Script as being merely an unusually complex manifestation of split personality. And to them the great psychic opposition we encountered is only a sort of sublimation of the persecution mania frequently met with in mental cases. Ye gods and little fishes!

But to revert to our proposed test. X is the ideal projectionist and his name is *not* Oliver Fox. X arranges with Dr. Z to visit the latter's study, which he has never seen, at 9 p.m. on a certain day. Dr. Z invites a clairvoyant and a materializing medium to be present in the room at the appointed hour, but does not tell them why they are wanted. The clairvoyant sees X (a stranger to him) enter the room, finger various articles, and read a book lying open on a table, etc., and then writes a full report of all he has seen. X then goes to the entranced medium and manifests through him, and a photograph is taken of X's materialized form. Finally, the next morning, Dr. Z receives X's written account of all that he did when out of his body, including a passage from the book, and this is found to agree in every detail with the clairvoyant's written report. Now such a test would, I think, be accepted by the majority of people as proof positive that X's soul had really left his body, but it would all be explained away quite easily by the enthusiastic adherents of the Subconscious Mind theory. Their position is simply unassailable; but whether such an attitude is a *reasonable* one, in the everyday use of the word, is a debatable point.

What is man ? a consciousness moving along a path in the four-dimensional space-time continuum ? Is his path predestined to the end ? Does his free will, seemingly negligible at first, become more and more perfect as he slowly and painfully—perhaps through countless "lives"—attains to union with the God within him, that infinitely precious Jewel of which I have spoken ? I am sometimes tempted to think that all such questions resolve themselves into one, which is of insuperable difficulty to our three-dimensional brains : What is time ?

It is almost forty years since my mother left me ; and save for those fragrant contacts in my dreams, I have received only one message from her in all that time. It did not come from her direct, but was transmitted— through automatic writing—by a celestial messenger. She speaks of her "residence in timeless places where the call of the hours is heard not at the door of the Soul".

This message was beautifully worded, and in many ways all that I could desire, and yet my heart sank as I read it. This new mother seemed so divinely remote, so far ahead of me in wisdom and knowledge, so celestially calm and "non-human", so utterly lost to that small boy who still exists in me. Here was a goddess, and I wanted the mother who used to laugh and run wild with the wind in her shining hair and jump tennis-nets. I wanted her to recall the day when she took me to Edmonton for a picnic and paddled in a stream and was startled by a frog. I can still hear the little scream she gave as it touched her leg. But she spoke of none of these dear trifles ; and even if she had, they would have possessed no evidential value. Yet near the end of her message she exclaims, "Oh, thy *time* !" And those three words struck home : there was my mother of long ago. For I could see again the charming, half-petulant movement of her head and her splendid eyes alight with mock indignation.

Sometimes I try an experiment that always fails. I visualize our sitting-room—the room where things "went wrong"—at Finsbury Park. I wear my sailor-suit and curl up in the comfortable depression in Daddy's armchair. On a table near by are his microscope, cigar-cabinet, the green china elephant which served as a receptacle for ashes, and a host of other objects— one by one I recall them. And there is the piano where my mother played duets with me, and our hands were four white horses galloping side by side. My toy pump stands on the window-sill, and it has made a rusty mark on the paintwork—there'll be trouble about that ! The *Strand Magazine* is on my mother's chair where she left it a few minutes ago. I can hear her moving about overhead. And on the ceiling is an incriminating patch, because I stood on the soap and upset my bath. No motor-horns sound in the Seven Sisters Road ; only the *clop clop* of the horses' hoofs, the rattle of wheels, and the jangle of harness and bells.

Now, surely, I shall hear a "click" in my brain, and I shall be *there*—back in the Past ? The door will open, and my mother will enter. But no—I cannot do it ! Always I fail. Of course I am unable to recall many of the objects in that over-crowded Victorian room. The pattern of the wallpaper eludes me. Carpet, hearthrug and tablecloth—even some of the pictures—I can't recall them, and yet they are all registered in some inaccessible region of my mind. If I could get it all back *perfectly*, would my magic work ? "Oh, thy *time* !"

With the possible—if doubtful—exception of the Theseus adventure and those dreams in which I may perchance have contacted the Eternal Records, the door of the Past has proved unyielding ; but the Future has opened, to some extent, many times. I have had a good number of dreams of the type Mr. J. W. Dunne deals with in his *An Experiment with Time* ; but they have all been trivial in nature or of small importance to me. The most striking experience I have had of a prophetic kind was not a dream, but a vision. Very shortly after I had met the lady who was to be my wife and before I had fallen in love with her— indeed, I think this happened at our third or fourth meeting—we were walking along the Western Shore beside the railway. It was a dark night and very quiet until an express rushed past us like a fiery dragon, the glow from the furnace being reflected in the trail of smoke. As I watched the line of lighted windows flashing past and heard the roar and rattle, quite suddenly a picture formed within my brain : just an ordinary sitting-room in which my companion and I were seated on either side of the hearth; and then I knew with absolute certainty that we were destined to marry. Being young and impetuous and considerably shaken by this sense of destiny, I promptly told her what I had seen. And she said nothing at all for a few minutes and then took up our conversation at the point where the train had interrupted. But she was obviously not offended. Some months later she told me that after our first meeting at a friend's house—although finding me too talkative and dogmatic to be attracted by me—she had suddenly felt with almost overwhelming force that she had met her fate. Indeed, the conviction was so strong she found herself trembling, and no wonder ! Yet on that occasion I had no sense of destiny and was not particularly interested in her, being too busy holding forth about my dream-research and Theosophy. So strangely do things happen.

Why is it that our spiritual experiences, like the roseate hues of early dawn, are so fleeting, so difficult to retain within the mind ? Swiftly the exaltation passes ; the memory becomes blurred ; we question its reality. Did that really happen ?

I have gone further than many people along a certain path. I have talked with Masters in another world. I have seen—though from afar—Celestial Beings, great shapes of dazzling flame, whose beauty filled the soul with anguished longing. And yet were it not for my records, the blessed written words—which ensure *permanence*, even though they veil and distort and make untrue—were it not for these, there are times when I should doubt *everything* ; yes, even the reality of my Master. So hard it is to kill the sceptic in me, nor do I want to altogether ; for scepticism is very useful as an aid to preserving mental equlibrium. As long as I can behave like a normal comfortably stupid person, it matters not though I be really mad as the proverbial hatter.

The ways of Celestial Beings are not the ways of mortals. Nearly ten years have passed since Azelda's last communication by the written word. Ten years! It seems a long time to me who wait ; yet it may be only the equivalent of a few months in her strange, incomprehensible, "timeless" existence. Yet, though no message comes to me, I have a sense of *nearness*. It is as though my Master and I lived in the same house together, but in separate rooms. No sound can penetrate those walls, nor are there any windows, but still I know that she is there. I am free to enter if I can solve the riddle of the intricate lock upon her door, but to do this I must understand Time and the Fourth Dimension. I can only wait and hope. One day the door may open and Azelda emerge from her so-long seclusion to make her wishes known. And I shall hear her voice again and see her calm, wise face.

What of the Last Projection ? There is nothing to fear. Be assured of that ! The terror is not in *us*, but in the body—the poor, frail, animal part, so weary, yet dreading its coming dissolution. We shall rise from that last sleep even as from some half-remembered dream of woe and feel those haunting shapes slip back into the night now past. Yes, young and strong again, shall we stand erect in the glamorous dawn of the new life, and stretch our spirit-arms to greet the glory of the rising sun.

My tale is told. Azelda shall speak the final words ; for I can think of no more fitting end than this quotation from her Golden Book :

"THE FAREWELL SONG OF THE SOUL

"When the last notes of the Summer Symphony steal through the garden, I shall prepare for a journey. I shall close the Book of Hours and set my seal thereupon with unfaltering hand.

"Never again from this window shall I see the chaste eastern maiden coming, rosy from slumber, or the argosy flying the Golden Fleece, sailing into the West.

"But I shall never forget them ; they are embalmed in the storehouse of Memory ; their gifts are preserved in the shrine of the Spirit.

"I shall need no gold for the journey : only the treasures of Love, the first-fruits of Sacrifice. Having not these, I must depart empty-handed.

"No creed writ on paper shall serve as a passport : only the Laws of Devotion—Right Thinking, Right Doing—engraven by the sculptor of Life on the scroll of the Heart.

"I shall take leave of those who have loved me. Their trembling words of farewell I shall cherish for ever. With my hand on the latch, smilingly shall I look back at them and give them my blessing.

"The land to which I travel is not distant. Though I move to a new house, we shall still be as neighbours. The hedge which divideth is not an impenetrable thicket ; it shall be pierced by the arrows of Love sped by a reverent desire.

"They shall hear my voice comforting them in the night of their sorrow. My hand shall clasp theirs on the helm when they steer over seas that are perilous.

"Then, when the Gong of Night striketh the amen to the Discourse of Time, I shall fling wide the door and go forth into the Dawn, singing.

"How shuttered and silent the house after my going !

None shall see me or hear me depart, save those having vision.

"Upon sandals winged as Thought shall I travel the roadway. I shall lift mine eyes unto the hills crested with glory. There, at the end of the journey, someone lovelier than the rose, tenderer than a mother, more understanding than the wise, will be waiting for me.

"My greeting, only these words : 'Is it thou, Love ?' In answer, only these : 'Come ! It is I !'

"Then in silence, after the seeking, the tilling, the sowing, after the watching, the sorrowing, the hoping, into the fields of Harvest shall we go hand in hand."